CHILDREN'S QUESTIONS: A MECHANISM FOR COGNITIVE DEVELOPMENT

Michelle M. Chouinard

WITH COMMENTARY BY
P.L. Harris
Michael P. Maratsos

W. Andrew Collins
Series Editor

MONOGRAPHS OF THE SOCIETY FOR RESEARCH IN CHILD DEVELOPMENT

Serial No. 286, Vol. 72, No. 1, 2007

 **Blackwell**
Publishing   *Boston, Massachusetts   Oxford, United Kingdom*

CHILDREN'S QUESTIONS: A MECHANISM FOR COGNITIVE DEVELOPMENT

CONTENTS

COMMENTARY

ABSTRACT

Preschoolers' questions may play an important role in cognitive development. When children encounter a problem with their current knowledge state (a gap in their knowledge, some ambiguity they do not know how to resolve, some inconsistency they have detected), asking a question allows them to get targeted information exactly when they need it. This information is available to them when they are particularly receptive to it, and because it comes as the result of their own disequilibrium, it may have depth of processing benefits. In that questions allow children to get information they need to move their knowledge structures closer to adult-like states, the ability to ask questions to gather needed information constitutes an efficient mechanism for cognitive development (referred to in this paper as the Information Requesting Mechanism [IRM]; this term is used because it includes question-asking and other information recruiting behaviors such as gestures, expressions, and vocalizations). However, the role of children's questions in their cognitive development has been largely overlooked.

If questions are a force in cognitive development, the following must be true: (1) children must actually ask questions that gather information; (2) children must receive informative answers to their questions if they are able to be of use to cognitive development; (3) children must be motivated to get the information they request, rather than asking questions for other purposes such as attention; (4) the questions children ask must be relevant and of potential use to their cognitive development; (5) we must see evidence that children's questions help them in some way—that is, that they can ask questions for a purpose, and use the information they receive purposefully to successfully achieve some change of knowledge state. This monograph reports data on these points.

Study 1 analyzed questions taken from four children's transcripts in the CHILDES database (age 1;2–5;1). This methodology allowed detailed, veridical analysis of every question asked by the children during their recording sessions. Results indicate that children ask many information-seeking questions and get informative answers. When they do not get an informative response, they keep asking; attention is not enough. Results also indicate that the content of children's questions parallel their conceptual advances, and shift within an exchange and over the course of development to reflect the learning process. So, these data suggest that the components of the IRM are in place and are used by children from very early in development, and the information they seek changes with time.

Study 2 asked whether preverbal children who are not yet asking linguistic questions can recruit information via gestures, expressions, and vocalizations, in addition to further investigating the linguistic questions of older children. This study analyzed questions from a cross-sectional diary study, kept by 68 parents of their children's questions (aged 1;0–5;0). Also, this methodology allowed for data collection over a large number of children, a large range of situational contexts, and allows for the collection of low frequency, high-salience events. Results from Study 2 suggest that all of the components of the IRM are in place, and extends these findings down to younger, preverbal children who recruit information using gesture and vocalizations.

Study 3 investigated the questions asked in one specific domain, biological knowledge, and examined the impact that different stimulus types have on children's questions. This study gathered data from 112 parent/child dyads (children aged 2, 3, and 4 years) walking through one of three zoos (one with real animals, one with drawings of animals, and one with three-dimensional replicas of animals), looking at the animals together. Results from this study also suggest that all of the components of the IRM are in place from the earliest age, further supporting the findings from Studies 1 and 2. In addition, while children still ask many nonbiological questions about the animals ("what is its name?"), biological information ("how do babies grow their bees?") is requested with much greater frequency in this study, although this need not necessarily be the case. Further, the nature of these questions suggests they may support the building of conceptual structures within the domain of biological knowledge, at a time just before the age when children make important conceptual changes in this area. Further, the type of stimulus materials used has an impact on the questions children ask; children are less likely to ask deep conceptual questions when looking at drawings or replicas of objects than when looking at the real thing.

Finally, Study 4 examines the causal relation between children's questions and change in knowledge state by investigating whether or not children can ask questions in order to gain information that allows them to solve a problem. Sixty-seven 4-year-olds were asked to figure out which of two items were hidden in a box. Half of the children were allowed to ask questions to help them figure this out. Despite many ways in which they could fail to use questions correctly, children who were allowed to ask questions were significantly more likely to identify the object hidden in the box, an overt indication of their change in knowledge state. Further, children relied on their existing conceptual information about the objects to help generate disambiguating questions; even though they had a faster "dumb" method of disambiguating the objects via nonconceptual perceptual information ("is it purple?"), they were just as likely to generate questions that tapped into nonvisible conceptual information ("does it purr?"). These results suggest that children are capable of using their existing knowledge structures to generate questions that change their knowledge state in a way that allows them to productively solve a problem; they further suggest that tapping into existing conceptual knowledge to help process a current situation, and use that knowledge to generate appropriate questions, is an integral part of question asking.

Together, the results of these four studies support the existence of the IRM as a way for children to learn about the world. Children ask information-seeking questions that are related in topic and structure to their cognitive development. Parents give answers to these questions, but when they do not, the children persist in asking for the information, suggesting that the goal of this behavior is to recruit needed information. The content of these questions shifts within exchanges and over the course of development in ways that reflect concept building. Finally, children generate questions efficiently in order to gather needed information, and then are able to use this information productively; they tap into their existing conceptual knowledge in order to do this. Thus, the ability to ask questions is a powerful tool that allows children to gather information they need in order to learn about the world and solve problems in it. Implications of this model for cognitive development are discussed.

I. INTRODUCTION

Traditionally the field of developmental psychology has had two primary goals: to describe development, and to explain development. So, while cognitive developmentalists try to describe what children know at a given age, they also want to know what mechanisms move children forward from one knowledge state to a more adult-like knowledge state. What processes and abilities allow children to move from where they are to where they need to be? The answer to this certainly involves many interacting factors, processes, and abilities. This *Monograph* examines one mechanism that has not been much explored: children's ability to ask questions to gather the information they need to build a more adult-like knowledge state.

How do children learn about the world? One part of the answer is that children are active learners who build better understandings of the world by exploring and manipulating objects. Piaget (1954) theorized that as children explore the world, they encounter new information that does not fit into their conceptual structures, and this results in "disequilibrium": a state of unresolved cognitive uncertainty that signals a problem. Disequilibrium is unsettling for children, and so they are motivated to reconcile this new information in order to regain equilibrium, and do so by either finding a way to fit the new information in with existing conceptual structures somehow, or by changing the existing conceptual structures to more accurately reflect the new information. Once an adequate solution is found and the information is processed, equilibrium is restored. Neo-Piagetians have reformulated Piaget's position somewhat, describing the child's exploration of the world as theory testing (Gopnik & Meltzoff, 1997; Gopnik, Meltzoff, & Kuhl, 1999; Gopnik & Wellman, 1994), where children have hypotheses that are tested and revised in light of new information that does not fit with current structures.

Like all good theories, this position leaves many issues to be explored. What about objects that children cannot fully explore on their own? Mountains, rainbows and stars seen in the distance cannot be touched, they can only be observed. Even with objects that can be touched, like cats or apples

1

or toasters, children can only gather so much information by themselves; they cannot discover why cats chase mice, how an apple comes into existence, or how the toaster gets so hot—but all of these pieces of information are necessary for us to really understand how cats and apples and toasters fit into our lives, and into the world around us. Harris (2000) makes this argument with respect to religious and metaphysical thinking, phenomena that children cannot possibly explore in a sensorimotor way, and have to explore internally in their imaginations. But even in cases when children are able to gather useful information on their own through sensorimotor exploration, it is not clear how the child comes up with initial "hypotheses," or how the child knows when to be conservative (to hold off changing the hypothesis until more evidence is gathered) and when to make adjustments to the hypothesis. And, importantly, it doesn't explain how the child knows what should replace an incorrect hypothesis—which of potentially limitless solutions do they try out now? The mechanisms that guide these choices are still largely missing from our understanding of cognitive development.

Many processes are likely involved in this; for example, Susan Carey (1999) has suggested that resolution of such problems "proceeds by trial and error, and involves processes such as abduction and inference to best explanation" (p. 322). But while children certainly use these processes, they alone still cannot explain what leads the child in one direction over another, or what helps the child avoid a potentially infinite failure to reach the right answer by trial and error. Does the child move through an infinite number of possible explanations at random until something happens to make sense? This hardly seems likely. So, what propels the child in the right direction?

Luckily, children do not have to solve these problems on their own; another part of the solution is that help is available in the form of more knowledgeable others. According to Vygotsky (1978), other people help children to learn by interacting with the child within the child's "zone of proximal development" (ZPD). The ZPD is the difference between what children can already do comfortably on their own and ". . . [their] potential development as determined through problem solving under adult guidance or in collaboration with more capable peers" (p. 86). Children have support from the other people around them; these people help them learn. But every parent has had the experience of trying to explain something to a child who just does not care to hear—just because the parent gives information to the child, even in the course of a shared situation, does not mean the child is going to be receptive to it and be able to make use of it in a valuable way.

However, children's active exploration of the world (either external or internal exploration) can combine with the rich sources of assistance that surround them, allowing them to elicit information that guides the direction of their conceptual development. We know that children look to adults as experts[1] for a variety of information about the world from a very early age, from information about what's safe and what is not via social referencing (Campos & Stenberg, 1981) to information about how to properly engage with a given object (Meltzoff, 1988a, 1988b, 1990). In fact, the ability to seek out information from our conspecifics seems to give us a particular evolutionary advantage, and allows us to learn efficiently (Tomasello, 1999a, 1999b; Harris, 2000). Questions are arguably a natural complement to this information recruitment; children can ask mom why the kitty chases that mouse, where the hot comes from in the toaster, or what that beautiful stripe of color across the sky is. Younger children who cannot yet form verbal questions might be able to gather information by pointing to unfamiliar objects, or holding them up to their parents quizzically. These inquiries would be no less informative than picking up an apple to experience how much weight it has, or hiding something behind a pillow and discovering that it does not disappear. They also would not be any less useful than the information that parents give to children unbidden—in fact, they may be more useful, because they help fill in blanks that are currently concerning the child. Asking such questions is a mechanism that can fill in gaps in the child's knowledge, help resolve internal disequilibrium, and—importantly—guide the direction of the child's thought, precisely when the child is trying to resolve such disequilibrium.

Why should questions be particularly useful to children during cognitive development in this way? Unlike information that children might come across while engaged by something else, or information that other people offer when children are not ready for it (information that might be ignored or misinterpreted based on the children's current conceptual structures), in theory children's questions get answers exactly when the children can use them most, when they are open to the information, and when they are trying to resolve a state of disequilibrium. Also, information that the child is ready for or interested in may make the biggest impression in terms of memory and cognitive organization; memory research has found that when new information is incorporated into a network of associations, it is much better remembered and utilized by the learner. For example, Bower and Clark (1969) found that subjects are better able to recall a list of words when they make up a story that incorporates those words (see also Dallett, 1964). Beyond the level of learning simple lists of words, learners are much better able to recall steps in a procedure if the activity is identified for subjects in advance (and thus the conceptual structure is up and being accessed); in other words, if they are told that a passage is about washing laundry, they will be better able to remember the steps that are specified in the procedure they read, as this information allows the learner to elaborate on what they are reading and fit it into existing conceptual structures as they go

3

(Bransford & Johnson, 1972). Further, a crucial factor here seems to be the active engagement of the learner (Burns, 1992; Hirshman & Bjork, 1988)—the act of generating a link for two words results in superior recall than being given a link for those two words generated by someone else (Bobrow & Bower, 1969). These studies all hearken back to the seminal study by Craik and Lockhart (1972) that argues that when information is processed more deeply, it is better recalled; these later studies have investigated which factors lead to greater depth of processing, and active engagement by the learner is a critical factor. Because of this, it's plausible that the self-generation of a question by an actively engaged child would show similar processing benefits for the information received in response to that question. Chouinard (2007) has found exactly this; in a within-subjects design that controls for the attention and engagement of the child, information that children received as the result of questions was significantly better remembered than information that was given to them unbidden. So, for such reasons, asking questions may be particularly useful for cognitive development.

How does this process of asking questions to build up knowledge work? The model presented in this monograph argues the following. The child is engaged with something, and brings an existing conceptual structure to the situation. For the purposes of this monograph, a conceptual structure is defined as some area of knowledge, such as a concept, category or domain, that consists of both particular facts (pieces of information, possibly learned in isolation, possibly even by rote memorization), and explanatory/predictive core principles that unite those facts and make predictions about them and the concept/category/domain in question. The child encounters some problem (i.e., incomplete knowledge, or a gap in knowledge; some contradiction in expectation or knowledge already in place; ambiguous information or circumstances), and this leads to a state of disequilibrium. This state motivates the child to ask a question to get information that can resolve the problem at hand. The response that the child receives gives information about which direction the knowledge state should now be pointed toward; the answer itself shows the child how to revise/reorganize the structure, or which new knowledge structure should be used as a replacement. This information is applied to the current knowledge structure, which is revised in light of the new information, whether that revision is just to add information that was missing (enrichment, sometimes referred to as the simple accumulation of facts/knowledge) or to reconceptualize the knowledge state in some way (conceptual reorganization, which involves a new organization of the conceptual structure, primarily through its explanatory core principles). The child then proceeds with the new knowledge structure, and sees how this works out. This process would begin with the child's earliest ability to recruit information, and would improve with respect to specificity as communicative abilities improve—gestures and preverbal communication (such as facial expressions and vocalizations) would easily be in place early enough to allow children in their earliest years to begin building the critical conceptual structures that will allow them to organize and understand the world, and would be supplemented by verbal abilities as the child moves forward into the toddler and preschool years.

Note that this does not mean children will learn everything they need to know all at once or that they will immediately achieve the right knowledge structure—they may have to go through stages of getting closer and closer to the fully adult-like knowledge state. For example, work by Vosniadou (1994) on how children come to understand that the world is spherical suggests that children may go through an interim step (or steps) on their way to adult understanding; upon being told that the world is round, children often resolve this piece of information with the conflicting information from their eyes that the world is flat and their presupposition that objects require support by deciding, for example, that "round" means shaped like a pancake—circular, but flat. When told that the world is a sphere, they may be able to revise their presupposition that objects require support, but may still be unable to reject the evidence of their eyes that the world is flat, and resolve this by deciding that the world must be a squashed sphere—generally spherical, but with flat sections on the top and bottom where people live.[2]

As children go through such revisions, questions may be an efficient way of reconciling new information and determining what needs to be revised in their thinking—which presupposition needs to be revised or abandoned, and which new hypothesis should replace the old one, helping children move from step to step. For example, in a collection of metaphysical questions asked by children, Harris (2000) presents a particularly memorable question from a 4-year-old boy, who asks "it is only the naughty people who are buried, isn't it, because auntie said all the good people went to heaven." He asked this because he had previously been told that good people go to heaven when they die, and he then walked by a graveyard where a burial was in process. Because he could see no way that the person is going to be able to get up through all of that dirt to make their way to heaven where good people go, the child uses logical processes and tries out what he thinks is the best explanation, concluding that the person must be naughty. He tests out his conclusion by asking the adult if this is so. Faced with this question, the adult can take the next step, and explain why the conclusion the child has drawn is not quite right, and provide information to lead him to the right way to think about the current issue.

Models of question-asking in the adult literature use a similar model to explain and predict question-asking in adult learners. The SWALE model (Schank, 1986) agues that adults generate questions when faced with an anomalous event, which leads to learning, and argues that much of long-term memory is built around a large set of previously experienced anomalous events that have been successfully explained. If this is so, it follows that the ability to resolve anomalous events by asking questions could be a powerful force for learning in children. The PREG model of adult question-asking put forth in Graesser and McMahen (1993) argues that cognitive disequilibrium underlies the information-seeking questions that adults ask. Graesser and Olde (2003) argue, "Questions are asked when individuals are confronted with obstacles to goals, anomalous events, contradictions, discrepancies, salient contrasts, obvious gaps in knowledge, expectation violations, and decisions that require discrimination among equally attractive alternatives. The answers to such questions are expected to restore equilibrium and homeostasis" (p. 524). So, in these models, question-asking is presented as a mechanism for learning in adults, in that it proposes that via this process, adults gather information needed to make necessary changes to their conceptual structures. The principles of this model also apply to children as described above, perhaps even more powerfully, as they seem to be strongly driven to resolve cognitive disequilibrium and have much more to learn about the world than adults; so, the ability to ask questions to restore equilibrium may be especially helpful in building up initial and subsequent conceptual structures by eliciting guidance when children are not sure which way to go.

QUESTIONS USED BY CHILDREN TO OBTAIN INFORMATION

What do we know about children's questions? Research into children's questions has so far had one of three objectives: (1) in the field of linguistics, to investigate the development of children's ability to form questions (when they begin to use question words, inversion techniques, etc.); (2) in the field of education, to investigate how question-asking can improve academic achievement; and (3) in the field of psychology, as a measure of what children know about a given domain of knowledge (and only as an index of knowledge, but critically not as an actual force in knowledge development itself). Objective 1 does not relate questions to children's knowledge development in any way, and so will not be reviewed here. Objectives 2 and 3, while they do not look at question-asking as a potential force for knowledge development in-and-of itself, are potentially relevant to knowledge development, and so will be reviewed below.

Work in the field of psychology, which has looked at children's questions as indexes of children's current knowledge states, helps us here. Sully (1896) reports on a diary of a boy, kept by his father, up to the age of 5;

among the observations are a smattering of questions from a range of areas, which are not analyzed in their own right, but are presented as a part of other phenomena being examined that run the gamut from the child's emotional, social, personality, and cognitive development. The questions that are reported are seen as giving insight into how the child sees the world at the time of the question; that is, Sully believed that the questions could help observers determine how the child was thinking about the phenomenon in question. However, the questions are not seen as a useful force in development in-and-of themselves. Sully sees his analysis of this diary as a selective commentary on salient aspects designed to highlight interesting phenomena, and not as conclusive data for anything; in fact he comments "if these do not always come up to the requirements of a rigidly scientific standard in respect to completeness, precision, and grave impartiality, they may none the less prove suggestive of serious scientific thought." The questions included in his paper do just that—whet the appetite to know more about the nature of the questions children ask, and how they relate to their cognitive development.

Piaget (1926) reports a diary study conducted over 10 months with a boy between the ages of 6 and 7 with the purpose of understanding the development of logic and causal explanation in children; questions (initially "why" questions only) were taken down intermittently by a female assistant during two-hour sessions designed for that purpose (and thus, conducted in extremely limited circumstances). Piaget does report many of these questions, but unfortunately does not report the answers that the child received, nor any other information about the linguistic exchange; this limits the use of these data for analysis. This is not surprising, because Piaget did not endorse the idea of knowledge acquisition through verbal transmission. So for him, the questions and the answers they elicited were not of any actual use to the child; for his purposes, these questions only allowed him to see how the child was thinking about phenomena in the world, and only that information was relevant.

Isaacs (1930) presents (in an appendix) an analysis of some "why" questions asked by early-elementary-aged children (actually primarily only one child) during a study conducted as the "Malting House Experiment in Progressive Education" between 1924 and 1927. He studies these questions because he believes they are evidence that children are actively interested in the world around them, and that this engagement, along with the internal state of processing information that goes along with it, leads to questions. He theorizes that "some fact that is contrary to expectation, or unexpected, creates confusion or difficulty as to what to expect next." He uses the questions he collected, and some he has found elsewhere, to illustrate this point. Interestingly, he is equivocal with respect to how much use these questions actually are to the children; he seems to see questions as a symptom of conceptual change, but not a force in it, saying "the instincts and needs it [question-asking] is called upon to help will not be helped by it. But it is there all the same to serve them, and it is sustained by them." The questions he discusses show a range of questioning behavior, and point to disparities as the source of questions in many cases in children, but he himself admits that the data are sparse in number and scope because of the nature of the study, that data recording was inadequate, and that the appendix is meant primarily as a theoretical thought piece.

None of these studies give insight into how these questions might be contributing to conceptual development—but this isn't surprising because that was not the purpose of these studies. One improvement on this (from the standpoint of this monograph) is a diary study by Callanan and Oakes (1992); the main purpose of their study was to use questions as a measure of whether or not preschoolers' concepts are embedded within causal theories about domains. At the end of each day for a 2-week period, mothers recalled and wrote down the questions their children had asked about causal issues throughout the day (questions about "how things work" and "why things happen"). They found that children's questions do indicate interest in causality across a number of domains. Further, these researchers also looked at the responses the mothers gave to their children, to see if these answers corresponded to such causal theories; they found that mothers give potentially useful information about causal mechanisms. Unfortunately, it is hard to know exactly what to conclude from this, because the study relies so heavily on parent's recall throughout the day; parents may recall answering questions they did not answer in fact, or may have had a tendency to answer questions they would not otherwise have answered because of the nature of the study. Further, there is no evidence that children use these answers in any way, or even take note of them, although again this is not surprising, because the main purpose of the study was not to look at how questions could be effecting conceptual change, but rather looked at these questions as a window through which the investigators could observe the children's conceptual structures.

A second improvement is work by Tizard and Hughes (1984). This study recorded the conversations of thirty 4-year-old girls (ages 3;9–4;3) each for one afternoon at home and two mornings at preschool. They found that the girls asked a wide range of questions, including "challenges," "business," and "curiosity." These authors argue that these questions could be a force in cognitive development, and present salient examples to argue for this point. While encouraging, these results are again difficult to draw conclusions from, based on the small recording sample and age-range of the girls, along with the limited analyses of the collected questions.

Education research has also looked at children's questions, with the goal of understanding how question-asking can improve academic achievement.

These studies suggest that questions asked by children in the classroom during formal education can have important benefits. Blank and Covington (1965) reported that increased question-asking was related to increased achievement by sixth graders (see also Schwabe, Olswant, & Krigsman, 1986). This benefit seems to come specifically from a child's self-generated question, rather than just any information being discussed in the classroom; Ross and Killey (1977) found that elementary school children recalled answers to their own questions better than answers to another child's questions. The reasons for these findings, however, remain underspecified, as the children may simply have been paying more attention at the time of their own questions (note that while this distinction is not important for the goal of the study, it is important for the goal of this manuscript, and will be addressed further below).

These researchers have also argued that elementary-aged children ask many different types of questions, including "wonderment" questions aimed at resolving discrepancies in knowledge, general questions designed to orient them to a topic, and questions asking for specific information (Berlyne & Frommer, 1966; Scardamalia & Bereiter, 1992). They also theorize that these questions come from epistemic curiosity such that when children need information to resolve some incomplete knowledge state, they ask more questions; note, however, that this may be a simple knee-jerk surprise response, and does not show evidence that children are intending to gather information, or that they use the information they receive in any way (similar to the argument made in Isaacs, 1930). Finally, one very encouraging study suggested that elementary-aged children can use questions to solve an immediate problem; Eiser (1976) found that third- through seventh-grade children were able to use a "twenty-questions" type game to gather information in order to solve a Piagetian-style spatial array task; here, older children at least, seem to ask questions effectively to gather information.

These studies are encouraging from the perspective of this monograph. They indicate a broad range of questioning behavior in a wide spectrum of areas. They suggest that questions may be useful for children, and that they may result from a state of disequilibration. In these ways, taken together, they hint at the possibility that question-asking may be a useful avenue available to children as they learn about the world. However, there are important limits that prevent us from being able to draw these conclusions from the existing literature.

In the case of the psychology studies, methodological problems limit the usefulness of the data. In these studies, data were gathered in a highly limited, scattered fashion, and only in certain predetermined situations. Data weren't gathered exactly due to the limitations of the technologies of the times. Only a small number of subjects were involved in most cases.

Because of this, the studies do not give information that allows any in-depth analysis of children's questioning behavior (this lack is true of the education literature, as well). How many questions do children ask? What type of content do children ask about? Are their questions such that they can be assisting conceptual development in some way? Do they get useful answers? Do they care about getting answers, or do they ask questions only to get attention, or as a knee-jerk reaction to something that captures their attention? What could they be learning, and how could these questions be playing a role in cognitive development? Of course, it is not surprising that this information is missing and that these analyses cannot be done, because that wasn't the goal of those studies. The goal of the work in this monograph is to go in a different direction, to investigate the role that questions play as a mechanism that aids cognitive development.

The goal of the education research is important to keep in mind for this reason, as well. Those studies were not designed to investigate the role that children's questions play in their cognitive development per se; questions were explored with respect to how they are correlated with school achievement. Their causal role is not of central importance; for example, the questions may have been epiphenomenal to the children's simply paying more attention to the topic at hand. Or children who are more engaged with a topic in the first place may be more likely to ask questions. What is important for these studies, and understandably so, is how to get children to learn most effectively, not the particular mechanism that underlies this gain.

One final problem with the existing literature is the age range of the target children. In most of these studies, the children are school-aged. This is particularly true of the education studies, which are of course done in school settings; while these studies show evidence that suggests asking questions aids school achievement, we cannot necessarily conclude that any such abilities shown by school-aged children have any relevance to conceptual development outside of the school setting. This is the case for two main reasons. First, we do not know if children's ability to ask questions in the classroom is something they have been taught by the school setting itself. The process of education itself often changes how children learn; mnemonic devices and other learning strategies taught in school make children more efficient learners inside and outside of the classroom. Using questions in a classroom setting, or learning to use them effectively, may similarly be a product of the educational system. Second, even if this question-asking ability comes from the children themselves and not the school setting, this ability may not be present in younger children. But by their first day of kindergarten (let alone fifth or sixth grade), children have already learned a considerable amount about the world, and have set up a complex set of conceptual structures. If questions are playing an important role in conceptual development, if asking them is a mechanism that aids conceptual

10

development, they would have to be of use much earlier than the school years.

This is a particular worry in light of findings that suggest limitations on even the older children's ability to even recognize that they need to ask for more information in some situations. Markman (1977, 1979) found that elementary-aged children often have a hard time knowing that directions they have just been given do not contain enough information for them to complete a task, and this is harder the younger the children are. Ironsmith and Whitehurst (1978) report a similar finding, showing that between kindergarten and fourth grade, children get better at asking for more information in ambiguous situations, with the younger children failing to do this. These failures may be due to the tasks that the children were given; for example, the Markman studies used reading/listening comprehension tasks to test the children's ability to detect ambiguity or insufficient information, but younger children do not normally learn about the world this way. Interestingly, when the children were required to act out the instructions, a situation much more analogous to how younger children interact with and learn about the world, they are able to detect that they do not have enough information, and ask questions. In the case of the Ironsmith and Whitehurst (1978) study, the "ambiguous" messages were messages where the information given could apply to more than one of the stimulus sets that the child had to select from; it is very likely that the younger children simply perseverated on the first item they found that fit the criterion, and chose that item rather than looking to see if the message (which they might reasonably expect to be informative enough coming from an adult stranger) applied to more than one item. Regardless of these possibilities, the fact remains that it is far from certain in the existing literature that even elementary-aged children are fully able to use questions efficiently to gather needed information; this concern would apply all the more to younger children with more limited abilities who thus might be even less skilled at using questions in a way that would aid their conceptual development.

SUMMARY AND GENERAL HYPOTHESES

To summarize, the model presented here argues that actively exploring children who have access to adult others to help guide their learning may use human communicative tendencies to gather information about the world. A smattering of data from several diary studies suggests that children may be asking questions that could assist cognitive development, but these data are severely limited and preclude any conclusions. Education studies with older school-aged children suggest that question-asking helps improve scholastic performance; however, these studies are limited in their controls and scope, and do not necessarily apply to younger children, who may not yet have the same abilities to use questions to gather information, or even recognize when they do not have enough information. More research is needed.

What do we need to know in order to claim that children's questions are a potentially important force in their cognitive development? The following must be true if question-asking is a useful mechanism for cognitive development:

(1) Children must actually ask questions. Therefore, the extent to which children ask questions, and how early they are able to gather information in this way, must be determined.

(2) Children must receive informative answers to their questions if they are to be of use to cognitive development.

(3) There must be evidence that the child wants to receive the information they are requesting, rather than simply wanting to get and keep the parent's attention, with no concern for the information requested.

(4) The questions children ask must be relevant to cognitive development; children must be asking questions to obtain information. If they are only asking questions that do not ask for information (but rather ask for in-the-moment permission to engage in certain activities, for example) they are of no use to conceptual development. Further, questions must be relevant to the content and processes of cognitive development; that is, they must obtain information that could be helping to meaningfully advance the underlying conceptual structures children rely on to organize the world and generate predictions about it. This would include both individual pieces of information and information regarding the explanatory core principles that underlie conceptual structures. These should also reflect the concepts that children are trying to work out.

(5) We must see evidence that children's questions help them in some way. That is, we need to see that they can ask questions for a purpose, and then use the information they receive purposefully, to successfully achieve some change of knowledge state.

This monograph presents four studies that gather evidence regarding these questions. Chapter II presents the findings from a longitudinal study of four children's questions, gathered from veridically recorded conversations.

Chapter III presents findings from a cross-sectional design examining the questions asked by 68 children over the course of a week. Chapter IV presents findings from a cross-sectional study involving the questions asked by 112 children on a specific topic: animals. Chapter V presents a study that examines children's ability to ask questions purposefully, in order to successfully achieve a desired goal. Finally, Chapter VI discusses these findings, and their implications for the existence and use of the IRM.

NOTES

1. The word "expert" as I am using it here refers to the fact that parents have more basic knowledge about how the world works than do children, and so are more "expert"; it does not involve advanced scientific knowledge such as an understanding of DNA or the molecular structure of gold, for example.

2. Recent work, such as Panagiotaki et al. (2003), challenges this model and suggests that children's knowledge may be less consistent than these results suggest. In light of this, however, these authors argue that children may be even more reliant on cultural information in forming their ideas about the shape of the earth than has been proposed before.

II. ANALYSIS OF THE CHILDES DATABASE

How many questions do children ask? Do they get answers to these questions? Are the children using questions to gather information? Is this information relevant to cognitive development? How does all of this change over the course of the children's development? Study 1 was designed to investigate these issues in a natural setting, following four children over the course of their development.

STUDY 1: METHODS

The goal of Study 1 was to compile a corpus of naturally occurring, spontaneous questions asked by children aged 1;2–5;2 years, with exact, detailed information about questions and responses, collected longitudinally over several children. The CHILDES database (MacWhinney & Snow, 1985) reports transcribed audiotapes of verbatim conversations between target children and adults; these conversations are recorded longitudinally, at regular intervals over several years of the child's development. With this database it is possible to gather an exact record of every question asked by the child during the recording sessions, along with the exact responses they received; this allows detailed, accurate analyses of frequency information alongside content information. This also allows us to follow changes in the same children's question-asking behaviors as they get older.

Participants and Procedure

Four children from the CHILDES database were analyzed ("Abe" from the Kuczaj corpus (2;4–3;11), "Adam" from the Brown corpus (2;3–4;10), "Naomi" from the Sachs corpus (1;2–4;9), and "Sarah" (2;3–5;1), also from the Brown corpus); these children were chosen because their transcripts were recorded regularly, because they covered the appropriate longitudinal age range, and because they represent a more diverse sample (although admittedly still very limited) with respect to subject demographics. Abe and Naomi were the children of psycholinguist parents who taped their language development in their home environment, during routine activities. Often these recordings took place during meals for Abe, and for both children, only the parent or parents were present, with a very rare occasional visitor. Adam was the child of well-educated, middle-class parents who were not professors, and who were black but who spoke standard American English rather than African American Vernacular English (AAVE). His recordings were made in his home, with multiple people present; in addition to his mother, 2 or 3 investigators were present for most sessions, often other adults such as his father or other adult relatives were present, in most sessions his baby brother was present, and in the later files, a foster child with behavioral problems was present (in other words, sessions were far from one-on-one). In addition, the investigators brought toys for Adam to play with during the session, so the focus of conversation was in large part centered around these toys. Most recordings were made just before lunch. Finally, Sarah came from a working class family, with only 1 or 2 investigators present (and on rare occasions, with none present). Sometimes other adults/children were present, but this was occasional rather than standard. Although the investigators did sometimes bring things for her, these were not the main focus of conversation. Recordings were made just before, or just after, lunch. With only four subjects, it is impossible to represent even all of the different groups that exist within American culture, let alone other cultures around the world. But as much as was possible using only four children, these corpora were chosen from those available to try to include different SES and racial backgrounds, as well as some variation in situational variables (i.e., number of people present, focused or free activity space). This information and the age range for each corpus is summarized in Table 1.

Data Coding

All questions asked by the children were extracted, along with the answer (or lack thereof) the question received; this resulted in a corpus of 24,741 questions. These questions were coded as noted below. It is important to note that during coding, the children's questions are considered in the on-going context, not in isolation, so a syntactically "incomplete" question (e.g., if the child is not yet using the word "why" or "how") can still be clearly asking for a particular sort of information, such as explanatory information. For example, during the assembly of a toy plane, the child might ask the procedural question "go there?" about where to put one of the pieces, or to ask how a toy got broken, the child might ask the explanatory

15

TABLE 1
DESCRIPTIVE INFORMATION ABOUT TRANSCRIPTS

Child	Age Range	Family	Present	Situation
Abe	2;4–3;11	European American, psycholinguist	Only child and parent(s) present	At home during routine activities, often during meals.
Adam	2;3–4;10	Black, well-educated, middle-class	Multiple adults and children present	At home before lunch. Investigators brought many toys which were often the center of attention.
Naomi	1;1–5;1	European American, psycholinguist	Only child and parent(s) present	At home during routine activities, usually before lunch.
Sarah	2;3–5;1	European American, working-class	Child, parent and 1–2 investigators present	At home before or after lunch. Investigators occasionally brought a toy for her.

question "daddy break?" So, from the time a child begins to speak, they are able to ask cognitively "complex" questions.

While on the surface such questions might seem to have many possible meanings, the context of the ongoing situation makes it possible to reliably determine the child's meaning. For example, if in the ongoing context we know that the toy is already broken, and that the father is not present, when the child asks "daddy break?" we know that the child cannot be asking the father to break a currently intact toy. We also know that the child is not asking the father to explain how the airplane was broken, because the father is not present (in other words, "daddy" is not used as a term of address here). Further, we know this is not an assertion on the part of the child, because the CHILDES database transcribes questioning intonation. So, logically, the child must be asking if daddy was the one who broke the plane. Because this ongoing situational information is so important to ensure accurate judgments of questions that were not syntactically well-formed, coders had to read the entire transcript rather than just looking at the question and one or two utterances before and after it. This was also necessary because the adult's response alone cannot be used to determine the nature of the question, as this would make any response analyses circular. To further address any problems with the relevant judgments, reliability was carefully tracked. All codes were trained to 95% agreement; all coding decisions were then made by two or more researchers, and all of the following codes tested at 95% reliability or higher. Questions were coded as shown in Table 2.

(1) General Question Type

Children ask questions for a variety of reasons, some that could be useful for cognitive development, and some that are not; because the purpose of this study is to examine questions that seek out information, children's questions were divided into information-seeking versus non-information-seeking questions. Definitions of these question types, along with examples, are found in Table 2. Noninformation-seeking questions have been further divided as noted in Table 2 below, to describe the full range of children's question use, but will not be examined further in this paper. Note that the division of information-seeking and noninformation-seeking questions used here is a conservative one that may underestimate the amount of information children are gathering. Arguably, a child who asks for permission to have a cookie or to go outside may be learning

TABLE 2

CODES FOR QUESTION TYPE

Question Type	Definition	Examples
Information-seeking questions		
Fact	Involves an isolated piece of information that does not contain a causal component	*What's that?* *Where's the ball?* *Do you like milk?*
Explanatory	Involves causal relation between objects and/or events	*Why is the baby crying?* *Why is the cereal hot?* *How come I cannot go outside?* *How do you draw a tic-tac-toe grid?* *How do you make it go over there?*
Noninformation-seeking questions		
Attention	Seeks attention from adult	*Hey mom?*
Clarification	Seeks to clarify what the adult just said	*What did you say?* *What?*
Action	Asks adult to take an action	*Can you fix this for me?* *Will you close the door?*
Permission	Seeks permission	*Can I have an apple?* *Can I go outside?*
Play	Addresses an inanimate object during play	*To doll: Are you hungry?*
Child/animal addressee	Addresses an animal or a baby who cannot answer	*To infant brother: Are you hungry?*
Unknown	Unable to determine	

something about when it is appropriate to eat cookies and when it is okay to go outside. However, this is not always the case; questions such as these also have a pragmatic aspect. In other words, children may know that they are allowed to go outside after lunch, but know that they cannot do so without making sure that mom knows where they are, and because of this, they have to ask permission. Similarly, asking if you can leave the table once you are done eating is often a formal part of the dinner process; both parent and child know when it is appropriate to leave the table, but this question and the answer mark a formal end to the meal. Further, permission often does not involve learning of the sort mentioned above but simply may be necessary due to moment-to-moment state of mind; the answer to the question "Can I sit in your lap" may sometimes be answered with a "yes" and sometimes with a "no," depending on what sort of mood dad is in. So, while trying to learn may be an aspect of some of these questions, this is not consistently the case, and it is better to be conservative by possibly losing some information here rather than to risk overestimating the questions that are motivated by trying to learn about the relevant situations and conditions in these cases.

In accord with the definition of knowledge structure used in this monograph, knowledge structures require two types of information; facts about a given category/concept/domain, and explanatory information that organizes those facts within the category/concept/domain. These two types of information-seeking questions have been coded separately, as shown in Table 2. This breakdown has empirical support in the literature; with respect to questions that could be useful for learning, research in the adult literature has argued that "shallow" questions (what I refer to as "facts") are asked by less-informed learners, while learners who already have knowledge on the topic at hand will ask "deep" (what I refer to as "explanatory") questions (Graesser & Olde, 2003). For example, when learning about locks, a less experienced learner may ask for the names of the lock parts ("shallow" questions), while more experienced learners will ask about how the parts are functioning ("deep" questions). While Graesser and Olde do not address developmental phenomena, for current purposes, it is important that questions that accumulate isolated facts ("what's this part called") are qualitatively different from questions that explore core explanatory principles and/or relationships between items, such as causal questions ("how does the key push the pins around?"). These questions may contribute differently to learning; for example, the former may contribute via enrichment of concepts, while the latter may lead to formation of underlying causal/explanatory principles.

These categories are mutually exclusive; each question was assigned to one category only.

(2) Question Content

These codes are designed to quantify the specific content of each question. The codes reported in this paper are designed to gather a data set about what general information children seek out about objects, people, and animals; these codes are listed in Table 3. The codes "label," "property," "appearance," "function," "part," "generalization," and "hierarchy" are designed to look more closely at what information children seek out during the categorization process, while learning what an object is and which new objects should be treated as part of a category. The codes "Theory of Mind (ToM)," "activity," and "possession" are designed specifically to investigate learning about people; importantly, however, all of these also apply to animals, and some can apply to objects, and an important part of the learning process is discovering which things apply to people only, or to people and animals but not objects and so on. The codes "state," "count," and "location" are designed to investigate transient states regarding objects and people.

TABLE 3

CONTENT CODES

Content Type	Asking About . . .	Examples
Label	The name for an object, or to what a name applies	*What's that?* *What's a jack-o-lantern?*
Appearance	A visible property of an object	*What color is it?*
Property	A permanent property of an object	*What is it made of?* *Is it soft?*
Function	The function of an object	*What does it do?*
Part	A part of an object	*Is that the donkey's ear?*
Activity	The activity of an object, person, or animal	*What is he doing?* *Is mom cooking?*
State	A temporary state of something	*Is it broken?* *Is he hungry?*
Count	The number of /the existence of something	*Is there any more milk?* *How many Legos are there?*
Possession	Who something belongs to, or if someone has possession of something	*Whose coffee is that?* *Do you have a cat at home?*
Location	Where something is or belongs	*Where is my ball?*
Hierarchy	How different category levels relate to one another	*Is that a poodle dog?* *What kind of car is that?*
Generalization	A category as a whole	*Do bats sleep upside down?* *Why do cats like milk?*
Theory of Mind	The beliefs, desires, knowledge, mental states, or personality of a person	*Do you want my milk?* *How does the pilot know where to fly the plane?* *Is he a mean dog?*

TABLE 4

CODES FOR RESPONSE TYPE

Response Type	Definition	Examples
Answered, information given	Adult gives information requested	*Question: What's that called?* *Answer: A grapefruit.*
Responded—information not given	Adult responds to child, but does not give information	*Question: What's that called?* *Answer: I don't know.* **[OR]** *Answer: Where did you put your spoon?*
Not answered	Adult does not respond at all	
Turned back to child	Adult asks the child to answer the question	*Question: What's that called?* *Answer: You know that, what's it called?*
Child answers own question	Child answers own question before anyone else does	*Question: What's that called?* *Child says: It's a grapefruit!*

These codes are not mutually exclusive. For example, a question might be about state of mind and an activity, for example "How come he does not like to run?"

(3) Response

Each question was coded with respect to the response, if any, it received, as shown in Table 4.

Some of these response types will be collapsed in the analyses below, but are noted here to demonstrate the full range of responses children receive. These categories are mutually exclusive.

(4) Additional Information

While linguistic limitations do not seem to keep children from asking different types of questions (see above discussion), they may still struggle to find the right way to ask for the specific information they need because they are not quite certain what it is they do not know about the issue at hand. In these cases, it is possible that parents supplement the information they give to children, adding information they believe is relevant to the current situation. For example, a child seeing a poodle for the first time may know what a dog is, but may have never have seen a dog that looks like a poodle before, and so may not even realize that it is a dog at all. The child may not realize, then, that the right question to ask is "what kind of dog is that?" and may rather ask "what's that?" The parent, knowing that the child knows what a

TABLE 5

EXAMPLES OF ADDITIONAL AND DIFFERENT INFORMATION GIVEN BY PARENTS

Response Type	Definition	Examples
Additional	Adult gives more information than the child requested	*Question: What's that?* *Answer: That's a dog. A poodle dog. He has a puffy tail.*
Different	Adult responds to the child informatively, but the information is different than what the child asked for	*Situation: Mother is shivering* *Question: What's mommy doing?* *Answer: She's cold.*

dog is, might answer, "It is a dog. It is a poodle dog. He has a puffy tail," to explain the situation for the child. To measure this, two codes were used to determine if the parent gave more information than the child asked for, or different information than the child asked for (if the child had phrased a question incorrectly, failing to correctly capture the phenomenon in question), shown in Table 5.

Note that in the second example here the parent is correctly reading the situation and identifying the phenomenon that is interesting to the child—the child wants to know what's happening with the mother, and the underlying issue here is that mom is cold. Both of these codes will be collapsed in the analysis but are noted here to demonstrate the ways that parents build on children's conceptual limitations.

(5) Isolated Questions Versus Series of Questions

As discussed above, children may need to learn different sorts of information (facts and explanatory principles, for example), and may need to learn some basic facts first in order to build up and learn further about a category. Children might ask questions in isolation, accumulating one piece of information at a time building only cumulatively over time, or they might ask multiple questions in a single exchange that build on each other (or both). Further, they might be more likely to ask for facts first, and then causal principles that relate these facts only after getting the initial facts (as seen in the Graesser & Olde, 2003, work where inexperienced adults first asked for basic facts, while experienced learners who already had those facts were able to ask questions that related those facts together). In order to examine the degree to which children ask isolated questions versus a series of questions related to one another, the number of questions asked in a row on a given topic was tracked. Also, the type of information requested at these different phases was tracked.

21

(6) Persistence

The number of times the child repeated the same question was tracked. Questions that varied in form but were asking for the same information were counted as the same question; for example, the question "what's that called" and "what's its name" would be treated as the same question.

In order to analyze differences on these dimensions in order to test hypotheses, frequencies were tabulated, and χ^2 analyses were performed to investigate significant differences.

DATA ANALYSIS AND RESULTS

Do Children Ask Questions, and Why?

Table 6 shows the number of questions asked by each child in the transcripts. The total data set comprises 24,741 questions, over 229.5 hours of conversation. This averages to 107 questions asked per hour by the children while engaged in conversation with adults; even in the case of the lowest per-hour average of 69 questions per hour, this sums to a considerable number of questions each day.

Why do children ask questions? If questions are a tool that assists cognitive development, they must ask for information about the world. Do children ask for information that could be helping them learn about the world, or do they only use this communicative device for other purposes, such as getting permission for activities? The breakdown by question type is shown in Table 7. This table shows that the majority of questions asked by children are information-seeking; the main purpose of their question-asking behavior, then, is to gather information. This function is a central aspect of this behavior.

Figure 1 shows the overall breakdown of information-seeking questions versus noninformation-seeking questions for each child; in each case, a

TABLE 6

NUMBER OF QUESTIONS ASKED BY EACH CHILD DURING TRANSCRIPTION

Child	Total Questions	Total Length of Corpus (Hours)	Questions Per Hour
Abe	5219	75	69.6
Adam	10,905	55	198
Naomi	2321	30*	77.4
Sarah	6296	69.5	90.6
Total	24,741	229.5	107.8

*This is an educated approximation based on the lengths of the files.

22

TABLE 7

PERCENT OF EACH QUESTION TYPE ASKED BY CHILDREN

Question Type	%	Question Type	%
Information-seeking questions	71	Noninformation-seeking questions	29
Fact (information-seeking)	56	Attention	6
Explanation (information-seeking)	15	Clarification	9
		Action	3
		Permission	5
		Play	1
		Child/animal addressee	1
		Unknown	4

question is significantly more likely to be information-seeking than to have another purpose, Abe, $\chi^2(1) = 12.96$, $p < .000$; Adam, $\chi^2(1) = 29.16$, $p < .000$; Naomi, $\chi^2(1) = 25$, $p < .000$; Sarah, $\chi^2(1) = 5.76$, $p < .016$. So, the primary[3] purpose of each child's question-asking behavior is to gather information about the world; the overall figure reported above is not an artifact of the combined data.[4]

However it is possible that children only ask information-seeking questions when they are older, and these questions are masking a lack of such questions at the younger ages measured. Figure 2 shows the breakdown of information-seeking and noninformation-seeking questions for the children at each age. Children's information-seeking questions constitute the majority of their questions; in every case at every age, a question is most

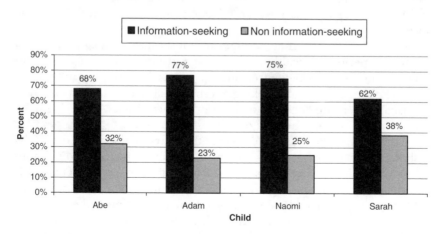

FIGURE 1.—Percentage of information-seeking and noninformation-seeking questions for each child.

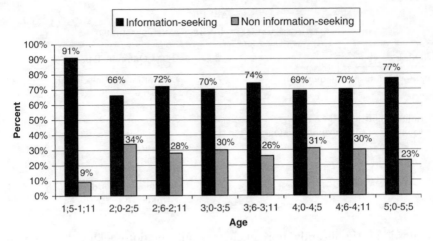

FIGURE 2.—Breakdown of question type at each age.

often significantly more likely to be an information-seeking question, 1;5–1;11, $\chi^2(1) = 69.59$, $p < .000$; 2;0–2;5, $\chi^2(1) = 10.24$, $p < .001$; 2;6–2;11, $\chi^2(1) = 19.36$, $p < .000$; 3;0–3;5, $\chi^2(1) = 16$, $p < .000$; 3;6–3;11, $\chi^2(1) = 23.04$, $p < .000$; 4;0–4;5, $\chi^2(1) = 14.44$, $p < .000$; 4;6–4;11, $\chi^2(1) = 16$, $p < .000$; 5;0–5;5, $\chi^2(1) = 29.16$, $p < .000$. So, from the earliest age, the mechanism is in place, and continues to be used by the children at every age: children have the ability to ask for information, and this is a central function of their questions. Across the ages, children show an increase in the percent of questions that are not information-seeking, Pearson's $\chi^2(7) = 21.735$, $p < .003$. However, this increase is accounted for primarily by the difference between the first two age groups, because almost all of the questions children asked at this age were information-seeking; when the analysis is performed without the first age group, there is no significant increase in noninformation-seeking questions, Pearson's $\chi^2(6) = 3.744$, $p = .711$. And, information-seeking questions still remain higher than non-information-seeking questions in all cases. So, across ages, gathering information is the primary function of children's questions.

How do these questions add up over the course of the child's day? Table 8 shows how many information-seeking questions are being asked per hour. When children are actively engaged with an adult, they ask an average of 76 information-seeking questions per hour; over time, these numbers would add up to a considerable amount of information being gathered by the child. So, not only do information-seeking questions comprise the majority of children's questions, cumulatively these questions are requesting a considerable amount of information throughout the course of cognitive

24

TABLE 8

NUMBER OF INFORMATION-SEEKING QUESTIONS ASKED BY CHILDREN DURING
TRANSCRIPTION

Child	Total Information-Seeking Questions	Total Length of Corpus (Hours)	Questions Per Hour
Abe	3526	75	47
Adam	8444	55	153.5
Naomi	1736	30*	57.9
Sarah	3916	69.5	56.3
Total	17,622	229.5	76.8

*This is an educated approximation based on the lengths of the files.

development. Question-asking is not something that happens every now and then—asking questions is a central part of what it means to be a child.

Do Children Get Responses to Their Information-Seeking Questions?

Asking for information is useless unless you get an answer to your question. Do children get answers to their questions that give them the information they are looking for? Figure 3 shows the percent of questions that receive answers containing the target information requested by the child. This calculation takes into account the child's persistence (which will be discussed later), meaning, if the child repeats the same question (for example, "Where's daddy") five times *in a row without an intervening topic change*, and receives an answer to only the fifth repetition, this would count

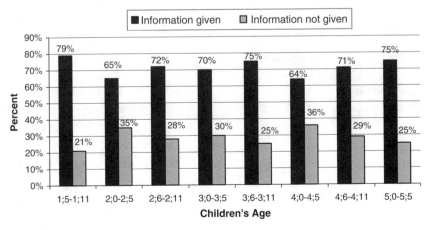

FIGURE 3.—Percentage of information-seeking questions that receive an eventual response.

25

as a 100% response rate to the question at hand. However, if the child asks "Where's daddy?" and does not receive a response, changes the topic, then returns to the previous question ("Where's daddy?") and then gets an answer, this would be treated as two separate questions, and would count as a 50% response rate.

This figure shows that at every age the child is significantly more likely to get the information they are looking for from the adult than not, 1;5–1;11, $\chi^2(1) = 33.64$, $p < .001$; 2;0–2;5, $\chi^2(1) = 9$, $p < .003$; 2;6–2;11, $\chi^2(1) = 19.36$, $p < .000$; 3;0–3;5, $\chi^2(1) = 16$, $p < .000$; 3;6–3;11, $\chi^2(1) = 25$, $p < .000$. 4;0–4;5, $\chi^2(1) = 7.84$, $p < .005$; 4;6–4;11, $\chi^2(1) = 17.64$, $p < .000$; 5;0–5;5, $\chi^2(1) = 25$, $p < .000$; in fact, in some cases they are three to four times as likely to get the information they ask for than to not get it. So parents interpret children's questions as serious attempts to get information, and children are successfully using questions to get the information they want from the adults they are interacting with. The likelihood of this stays the same over the course of development; the children are just as likely to receive a response at every age, Pearson's $\chi^2(7) = 8.902$, $p = .260$. Here again, the mechanism is in place from the start, and remains in place, allowing children to recruit information successfully.

As noted in the coding categories above, while children do not seem to be limited in the types of questions they can ask (fact, explanation), children may not know what specific information is relevant to the situation at hand, as shown in the poodle and shivering examples in the section above. This is particularly true of younger children, who have less of a conceptual base to draw on. We might expect, then, that when parents do answer a question, they may compensate for their child's limits by offering additional information that may help the child understand the topic at hand more

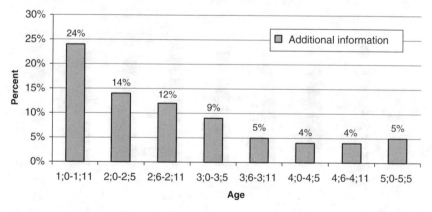

FIGURE 4.—Percent of informative responses to children's questions that contain additional information.

26

completely. Figure 4 shows how often parents offered additional information to children, above and beyond that asked for by the child.

For all of the children, parents provide additional information to supplement children's questions, ranging from 1% to 24% of the time. As predicted, parents give more additional information to younger children, Pearson's $\chi^2(7) = 38.84$, $p < .000$; so, in addition to answering the lion's share of their children's questions, they also add additional information to help their children along, particularly when their children are younger and need more assistance. Children's questions open the door, allowing parents to guide their children's thinking.

Are certain types of questions more likely to receive additional information than others? For example, is a question that asks for a fact more likely to receive additional information than a question that asks for an explanation? We will return to this issue below.

How Persistent Are Children at Getting the Information They Are Requesting?

Of course, just because children ask questions and get informative answers does not mean they actually care about the information in the first place—it's possible that they are only asking the question mindlessly, and would not even notice if they did not get a response. It is also possible that children just want to get their parent's attention, and are happy with any response they get, even if it does not contain the requested information; maybe they don't really care about getting the information at hand. Finally, children may just like to ask questions, and may keep parroting them even when they do get the information they requested. A way to differentiate these possibilities is to look only at cases where children do get a response (and therefore, get the parent's attention), and compare the rates of persistence in these cases to how often they repeat their question when parents give an informative answer (one that contains the target information *and* attention). If children simply want attention, we'd predict that when children receive a response from the parent that does not contain the information they asked for they'd be just as happy as when they receive a response that does contain the information they asked for and we'd expect to see low levels of persistence in both cases. If children just enjoy repeating questions, and are parroting them even when they have already gotten the information they ask for, we'd expect to see high levels of persistence in both cases. However, if children are purposefully using questions to gather information and resolve some internal state of disequilibrium, we'd expect them to be dissatisfied if they do not get the information, and to continue trying to get it; in this case, they'd be concerned with getting the information they ask for, and we would expect to see higher levels of persistence when they got a response that did not contain the information, and low

27

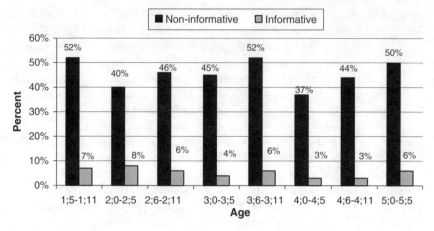

FIGURE 5.—Children's persistence after noninformative responses versus informative responses.

levels of persistence when they receive a response that does contain the target information. Figure 5 shows that the last is exactly what we find; This figure shows overwhelmingly that when children get a response from the parent that does not contain the target information, they are significantly more likely to repeat their question than when they've received a response that does contain the information, 1;5–1;11, $\chi^2(1) = 34.32$, $p < .000$; 2;0–2;5, $\chi^2(1) = 21.33$, $p < .000$; 2;6–3;0, $\chi^2(1) = 30.77$, $p < .000$; 3;0–3;5, $\chi^2(1) = 34.30$, $p < .000$; 3;6–3;11, $\chi^2(1) = 36.48$, $p < .000$; 4;0–4;5, $\chi^2(1) = 28.80$, $p < .000$; 4;6–4;11, $\chi^2(1) = 35.77$, $p < .000$; 5;0–5;5, $\chi^2(1) = 34.57$, $p < .000$. This tendency does not change with age, Pearson's $\chi^2(7) = 3.634$, $p = .821$. So, children are not asking these questions simply to get attention, nor are they simply enjoying repeating the same question over and over again; these analyses suggest that children are asking questions for the purpose of getting information. They continue to ask the question until they get the information needed to restore internal equilibrium, and once they accomplish this, they stop asking the question. This strongly suggests that their primary purpose for asking information-seeking questions is to get the information from the earliest age.

Also, we'd like to know that this pattern of persistence is particular to questions, and is not just some general pattern of repetition across all conversational turns; an attempt to get information should be privileged in this way. When children make a statement that is not followed by a response that addresses the topic at hand, do they repeat their comment until it is acknowledged by an on-topic response? In other words, are they just as persistent about making sure their utterance is addressed with an on-topic response when it is a nonquestion statement as when it is a question?

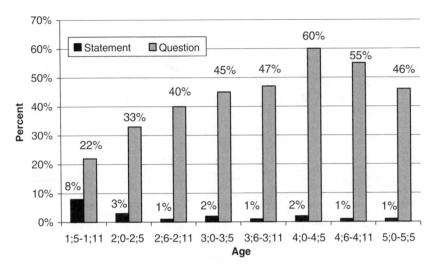

FIGURE 6.—Percentage of statements repeated versus questions repeated at each age.

Figure 6 shows that this is not the case; at every age, children are significantly more likely to repeat a nonanswered question than to repeat a nonanswered statement, 1;5–1;11, $\chi^2(1) = 6.533$, $p < .011$; 2;0–2;5, $\chi^2(1) = 25$, $p < .000$; 2;6–2;11, $\chi^2(1) = 37.10$, $p < .000$; 3;0–3;5, $\chi^2(1) = 39.34$, $p < .000$; 3;6–3;11, $\chi^2(1) = 44.08$, $p < .000$; 4;0–4;5, $\chi^2(1) = 54.26$, $p < .000$; 4;6–4;11, $\chi^2(1) = 52.07$, $p < .000$; 5;0–5;5, $\chi^2(1) = 43.09$, $p < .000$. So, children are particularly sensitive to getting a response that addresses the content of their questions; they are much less concerned with getting a response that addresses other conversational turns. This suggests that questions are fulfilling a different role than other aspects of conversation—specifically, they gather information that children want or need, and if that function is not fulfilled, children will keep trying until it is.

What General Type of Information Do Children Ask For?

Facts Versus Explanatory Principles

What sorts of information do children ask for? Are they asking for isolated facts, or for explanatory information? Conceptual structures contain both a set of related and relevant facts, and a set of underlying explanatory principles that allow children to relate these facts to one another, and make predictions about the concept at hand and how it relates to the world and other concepts. For example, an understanding of biology might include knowing the fact that a plant is considered alive, but also includes understanding that being alive requires maintenance of a life cycle; this

29

understanding allows the child to predict that anything that is alive needs fuel, and that any living creature that fails to take in fuel will die. Together the above underlying principle (living things must maintain a life cycle) along with the above fact (plants are alive) allow the child to predict that plants need to take in fuel to live.

As adults learn about a given topic, the questions they ask shift from more "shallow" (fact) questions to more "deep" (explanatory) questions (Graesser & Olde, 2003). This shift is an indication that learning is taking place, and that the individual is building up knowledge about a concept/category/domain. In accord with this, we would expect children to ask both for isolated facts, and to seek deeper causal/explanatory understanding about the topic at hand. Further, we would expect to see a shift in emphasis as children learn, moving toward more explanatory information as they are trying to relate a system of accumulated facts. We would expect to see this at both a micro level (within a single exchange) and a macro level (over several different exchanges over time). In other words, as children get older, we'd expect to see them asking more explanatory questions; we would also expect that within a single series of questions at a given time about a topic we would expect the first questions to be fact questions, with a shift toward explanatory questions further within the exchange.

Figure 7 shows how the proportions of fact and explanatory questions that children request changes over the course of the preschool years. The majority of information children request at all ages are fact questions. However, the percentages of explanatory questions increase over time, as predicted, Pearson's $\chi^2(7) = 53.05$, $p < .000$. So, as children get older, they

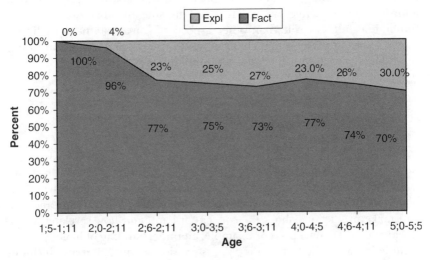

FIGURE 7.—Percent of each general category in the children's questions.

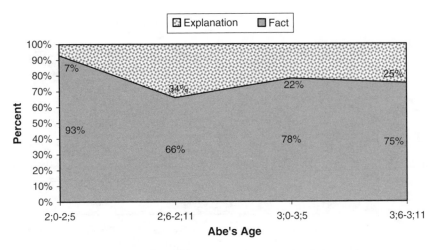

FIGURE 8.—Percent of each general category in Abe's questions.

are asking more for information that relates the facts they've learned about a concept.

This figure also hints at an interesting individual trend. There is a steep increase in explanatory questions at the third age group, 2;6–2;11, and a slight drop-off between the fifth and sixth age group (3;6–3;11 and 4;0–4;5), before the data starts to increase again. What might be happening here? This may be a meaningless data blip, but when we look at the data from each individual child, we find a more dramatic version of the same trend in each child's data: a spike in explanatory questions. This spike occurs for Abe at 2;6–3;0, for Adam at 3;6–3;11, for Naomi at 3;0–3;5, and for Sarah at 3;0–3;5), as seen in Figures 8–11. This spike seems to indicate

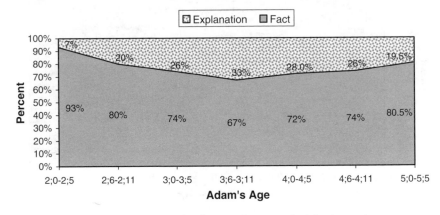

FIGURE 9.—Percent of each general category in Adam's questions.

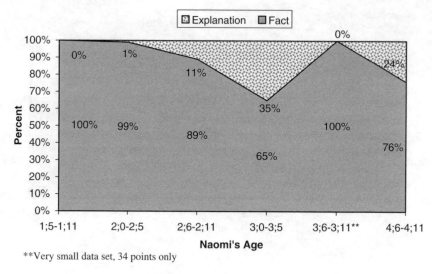

**Very small data set, 34 points only

FIGURE 10.—Percent of each general category in Naomi's questions.

an "a-ha" period, where children are particularly interested in causal principles. These increases are higher than both the age before and after them, although the difference between the spike and the age after it is slightly more subtle, due to the overall increase in explanation/procedural questions that is happening over the age trend, Abe, 2;0–2;5 versus 2;6–2;11, Pearson's $\chi^2(1) = 20.676$, $p < .000$; 2;6–2;11 versus 3;0–3;5, Pearson's

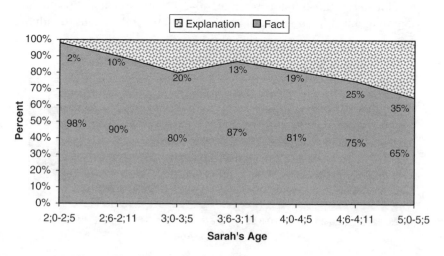

FIGURE 11.—Percent of each general category in Sarah's questions.

32

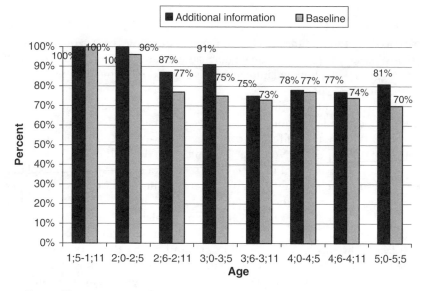

FIGURE 12.—Percentage of questions receiving additional information that asks for facts at each age.

$\chi^2(1) = 3.571, p = .059$, trend approaching significance; Adam, 3;0–3;5 versus 3;6–3;11, Pearson's $\chi^2(1) = 21.13$, $p < .000$; 3;6–3;11 versus 4;0–4;5, Pearson's $\chi^2(1) = 5.094, p < .024$; Naomi, 2;6–2;11 versus 3;0–3;5, Pearson's $\chi^2(1) = 39.16$, $p < .000$; 3;0–3;5 versus 3;6–3;11, Pearson's $\chi^2(1) = 39.16$, $p < .000$; Sarah, 2;6–2;11 versus 3;0–3;5, Pearson's $\chi^2(1) = 16.55$, $p < .000$; 3;0–3;5 versus 3;6–3;11, Pearson's $\chi^2(1) = 1.78$, $p = .182$, trend approaching significance. During this time, children may be making particular progress with causal understandings of many facts they've before accepted without question; however, this is pure speculation, and further research would be necessary to confirm what exactly is happening during this "a-ha" period.

Let's return for a moment to the questions children ask that receive additional information from the parents. It is possible that parents offer additional information selectively to only certain types of questions, for example, when the child asks a fact question, but are less likely to do so when the child asks an explanation question. Figure 12 shows what percent of the questions that received additional information from the adult were fact questions, compared with the baseline rate of fact questions at each age (the baseline is shown in Figure 7); this figure shows that at each age, the percent of fact questions that received additional information is the same as the baseline percent of fact questions asked by children, 1;5–1;11, $\chi^2(1) = .000$, $p = 1$; 2;0–2;5, $\chi^2(1) = .082, p = .775$; 2;6–2;11, $\chi^2(1) = .610, p = .435$; 3;0–3;5,

$\chi^2(1) = 1.542, p = .214;$ 3;6–3;11, $\chi^2(1) = .027, p = .869;$ 4;0–4;5, $\chi^2(1) = .006,$ $p = .936;$ 4;6–4;11, $\chi^2(1) = .060, p = .807;$ 5;0–5;5, $\chi^2(1) = .801, p = .371.$ So, parents do not show differential attention to one of these types of questions, but are just as likely to give additional information to any question the child asked; this suggests that additional information is dictated more by the situation than by the question type.

Returning to the main analysis, as predicted, on the macro level children are accumulating both a store of facts, and are increasingly interested in relating this system of facts through explanatory core principles over the course of development. Note that this shift is not due to the child's changing linguistic ability; as noted in the coding section, a child can ask an explanatory question before knowing the relevant question words or syntactic structures. So, a child who asks "daddy broke?" while looking at a broken toy airplane is perfectly capable of eliciting explanatory information about what caused the airplane to be broken early on in linguistic development, and lack of linguistic skills, therefore, is not limiting the type of questions asked early on. Because this change in focus is not due to those limitations, these data suggest some aspect of conceptual development is fueling this change.

What happens at the micro level, within a series of questions that are asked about the same topic at the same time? First we need to know if children even ask series of questions on topics that could build in this way (henceforth "building exchanges"); it is possible that they only ask isolated questions. Figure 13 examines how many questions asked by the children

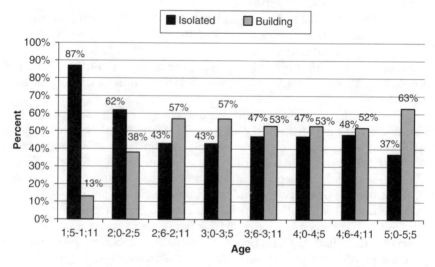

FIGURE 13.—Percentage of children's questions that are isolated versus building.

are single questions only (isolated), or are part of a building exchange that involves more than one question. While isolated questions are common at all ages, approximately one-third to two-thirds of children's questions build on each other, occurring in exchanges of more than one question, except in the case of the very youngest age group; while this percent is smaller than that seen in the older ages, it shows that even the youngest children still ask questions that work together to build on one another. Building questions increase with age (Pearson's $\chi^2(7) = 71.19$, $p < .000$); this change is not fueled solely by the difference between the first and second ages, but holds up even when we consider only the data from age groups 2–8 (Pearson's $\chi^2(7) = 14.36$, $p < .026$). So, starting young, children are already asking series of questions that work together to learn about a topic at hand, and their skill in doing this increases as they get older; we would expect to see these building exchanges if children are relating facts and explanatory principles as they get older.

Second, we need to know what happens within these exchanges. If children are accumulating facts and then focusing on relating them through explanatory information as predicted, we'd expect the first questions children ask to be fact questions, and expect that questions that come later in an exchange would be more likely to ask for explanatory information; that is, isolated questions or initial questions within building exchanges would be less likely to ask for explanatory information than questions that come later in the building exchange. Figure 14 shows this is what we find.[5] After age 2;5, a question that builds within an exchange (a question that occurs after a first

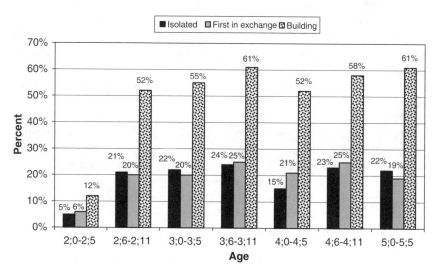

FIGURE 14.—Percentage of children's isolated versus building questions that are explanation questions.

initial question) is significantly more likely to ask for explanatory information than a question that is isolated, 2;0–2;5, $\chi^2(1) = 2.88$, $p = .090$; 2;6–2;11, $\chi^2(1) = 13.16$, $p < .000$; 3;0–3;5, $\chi^2(1) = 14.14$, $p < .000$; 3;6–3;11, $\chi^2 = 16.11$, $p < .000$; 4;0–4;5, $\chi^2(1) = 20.43$, $p < .000$; 4;6–4;11, $\chi^2(1) = 15.12$, $p < .000$; 5;0–5;5, $\chi^2(1) = 18.33$, $p < .000$, or than a question that is the first question in an exchange, 2;0–2;5, $\chi^2(1) = 2$, $p = .157$; 2;6–2;11, $\chi^2(1) = 14.22$, $p < .000$; 3;0–3;5, $\chi^2(1) = 16.33$, $p < .000$; 3;6–3;11, $\chi^2 = 15.07$, $p < .000$; 4;0–4;5, $\chi^2(1) = 13.16$, $p < .000$; 4;6–4;11, $\chi^2(1) = 13.12$, $p < .000$; 5;0–5;5, $\chi^2(1) = 22.05$, $p < .000$. At the first age, the trend is in the same direction, with a building question being twice as likely as an isolated or a first question to ask for explanatory information, but this trend does not reach significance. In light of the developmental finding that explanatory questions are less common at younger ages, it is not surprising that this fails to reach significance, because very few questions are asking for explanatory information in any case at this age.

Does children's ability to build up conceptual information over the course of a single exchange change with age? There is no significant difference over the ages in these data (Building vs. Isolated: Pearson's $\chi^2(6) = 1.11$, $p = .981$; Building vs. First: Pearson's $\chi^2(6) = 1.30$, $p = .972$). So, children's ability to build up conceptual structures in this way is another crucial aspect of the mechanism that is in place very early on.

In addition, an isolated question is no more likely to ask for explanatory information than the first question in a building exchange, or vice versa, 2;0–2;5, $\chi^2(1) = .091$, $p = .763$; 2;6–2;11, $\chi^2(1) = .024$, $p = .876$; 3;0–3;5, $\chi^2(1) = .095$, $p = .758$; 3;6–3;11, $\chi^2 = .020$, $p = .886$; 4;0–4;5, $\chi^2(1) = 1$, $p = .317$; 4;6–4;11, $\chi^2(1) = .083$, $p = .773$; 5;0–5;0, $\chi^2(1) = .220$, $p = .639$. This suggests that the first question in an exchange is functioning in the same way as an isolated question; what differs is that in the case of building exchanges, the child follows up the starting point by elaborating with further questions, while in the case of isolated questions, the child does not elaborate further. This does not change with age, Pearson's $\chi^2(2) = 1.474$, $p = .961$.

Note that the progression from fact question to explanatory question here cannot be due to any difference in cognitive ability. The same child is asking both types of questions within the same exchange, within moments of one another. And in further exchanges, the progression is the same, from fact to explanatory information. So, the later occurrence of explanatory questions within the exchange cannot be due to a change in the child's cognitive ability (such as the ability to think in causal terms, for example).

Overall, then, the data strongly confirm the prediction that children start out an exchange asking for facts, and shift their focus towards explanatory information farther into the exchange. So, this progression of complexity occurs within an exchange as well as over the course of their development; these patterns bear out the predictions based on the shift seen as adult learners move from novice to more expert on a topic.

What Content Do Children Ask About?

What specific types of information do children ask for? To explore what interests children as they are learning about and categorizing objects, animals and people, this finer-grained analysis looks at the specific information children requested. Tables 9–13 show the results of these analyses with the relevant percentages; Figures 15 and 16 show the trends in the overall data in a linear format for ease of reading. There is surprising consistency across the four children with respect to the questions they are asking. For each child, appearance, property, part, count, possession, hierarchy, and generalization questions were infrequent, and remained relatively stable over time. Questions about function, activities, ToM, state and identity were a larger proportion of the child's questions, and increased over time. Finally, questions asking for labels and location started out comprising a large percentage of the children's questions, and decreased over time; this is particularly true of questions asking for labels (further proof that children are asking first for basic facts such as labels before shifting towards fleshing out categories and explanatory principles more fully). Table 9 shows the data averaged over all four children, with the individual charts for each child following in Tables 10–13.[6]

Two of these content types in particular correspond compellingly to the timing of two of the cognitive advances we know children to be making; these are highlighted in Figure 17. Children start to go through the vocabulary spurt roughly between the ages of 1;0–1;3, and come out of the vocabulary spurt roughly between ages 2;0 and 2;5 (Benedict, 1979; Goldfield & Reznick, 1990). Children are asking for labels most frequently during the times that correspond to the vocabulary spurt, and are asking fewer questions at the time that they are coming out of the vocabulary spurt, Pearson's $\chi^2(7) = 121.32, p < .000$. We see the opposite trend with respect to ToM. As children get older, their understanding of other people's minds increases, and their ToM becomes increasingly complex and nuanced as they get older. For example, younger children have difficulty understanding that people can believe something that is false; 3-year-olds have a difficult time with this concept while 5-year-olds understand it (Gopnik & Astington, 1988). Still other aspects of ToM take even longer to achieve; children have a hard time with metacognition (such as knowing when and how people learn), achieving some understanding here between the ages of 4 and 5, with some advances not taking place until 7 or 8 (Flavell, 1999; Flavell, Green, & Flavell, 1995). In accord with this, we see

TABLE 9

Percentage of Each Question Type Over All the Children's Questions

	Appearance	Property	Part	Function	Activity	ToM	State	Count	Label	Possession	Location	Hierarchy	Generalization	Identity
1;5–1;11	2	2	3	2	9	0	6	.3	61	.3	24	0	1	3
2;0–2;5	1	2	3	2	18	2	6	2	41	3	24	.1	.1	8
2;6–2;11	1	3	4	4	27	10	11	2	20	7	26	1	1	13
3;0–3;5	1	4	4	6	33	14	15	2	15	5	22	2	1	16
3;6–3;11	2	6	4	7	31	11	15	2	16	4	19	1	3	14
4;0–4;5	3	7	4	12	24	13	12	3	13	5	14	.3	1	11
4;6–4;11	2	8	4	8	25	17	14	3	12	6	13	1	1	13
5;0–5;5	7	6	4	13	37	12	15	4	13	4	16	0	1	9

ToM, Theory of Mind.

TABLE 10

Percentage of Each Question Type in Abe's Questions

	Appearance	Property	Part	Function	Activity	ToM	State	Count	Label	Possession	Location	Hierarchy	Generalization	Identity
1;5–1;11														
2;0–2;5	0	0	3	9	18	4	1	1	28	11	7	3	1	33
2;6–2;11	2	4	4	6	36	6	11	2	14	10	22	1	1	13
3;0–3;5	2	7	5	9	35	8	15	3	11	5	23	1	3	16
3;6–3;11	1	9	1	6	42	16	14	4	9	5	14	3	3	13
4;0–4;5														
4;6–4;11														
5;0–5;5														

ToM, Theory of Mind.

TABLE 11

PERCENTAGE OF EACH QUESTION TYPE IN ADAM'S QUESTIONS

	Appearance	Property	Part	Function	Activity	ToM	State	Count	Label	Possession	Location	Hierarchy	Generalization	Identity
1;5–;11														
2;0–2;5	1	3	2	3	11	2	8	2	39	3	29	.1	0	7
2;6–2;11	1	3	4	2	25	16	12	1	20	6	28	.4	.1	11
3;0–3;5	1	4	4	6	34	17	16	2	18	5	20	2	.3	16
3;6–3;11	1	5	5	8	25	6	17	2	24	4	17	1	3	11
4;0–4;5	1	6	5	16	27	12	13	3	10	7	17	.3	1	12
4;6–4;11	2	9	4	10	20	17	14	3	14	7	15	2	1	12
5;0–5;5	2	7	5	9	25	22	10	1	14	10	17	0	0	16

ToM, Theory of Mind.

TABLE 12

PERCENTAGE OF EACH QUESTION TYPE IN NAOMI'S QUESTIONS

	Appearance	Property	Part	Function	Activity	ToM	State	Count	Label	Possession	Location	Hierarchy	Generalization	Identity
1;5–1;11	2	2	3	2	9	0	6	.3	61	.3	24	0	1	3
2;0–2;5	2	.4	4	1	35	2	5	0	35	4	25	0	.2	9
2;6–2;11	0	4	1	4	20	2	4	1	34	5	23	0	.3	22
3;0–3;5	4	1	1	1	14	20	2	.7	15	2	21	0	.7	17
3;6–3;11	13	6	29	16	3	0	0	0	23	0	39	0	0	13
4;6–4;11	0	0	7	9	38	25	14	0	25	4	26	12	2	5
5;0–5;5														

ToM, Theory of Mind.

TABLE 13

PERCENTAGE OF EACH QUESTION TYPE IN SARAH'S QUESTIONS

	Appearance	Property	Part	Function	Activity	ToM	State	Count	Label	Possession	Location	Hierarchy	Generalization	Identity
1;5–1;11														
2;0–2;5	0	1	4	.3	3	0	5	4	65	2	16	0	0	4
2;6–2;11	2	2	5	3	15	9	7	2	22	3	29	0	0	14
3;0–3;5	2	1	4	4	25	6	7	2	9	6	34	.3	1	20
3;6–3;11	3	5	4	4	24	12	14	1	8	4	37	1	.3	24
4;0–4;5	4	8	3	10	21	14	12	3	15	4	12	.3	.5	11
4;6–4;11	3	8	4	6	29	17	14	3	9	4	10	.2	1	15
5;0–5;5	1	6	8	14	41	8	17	6	12	2	18	0	1	6

ToM, Theory of Mind.

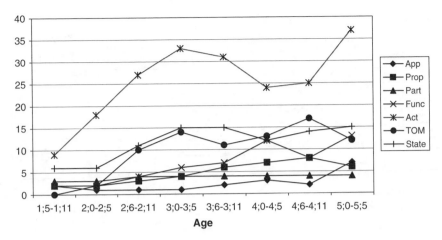

FIGURE 15.—Percentage of appearance-state questions over all the children's questions.

an increase in ToM questions as the children are getting older, when we know them to be working through more advances in ToM, Pearson's $\chi^2(7) = 24.89$, $p < .001$. The questions examined here, then, seem to be tapping into something about how children are thinking about the world, and the puzzles they are working out; when they are working out issues in an area, their questions increase accordingly. In light of these correspondences, other information contained here, such as the children's focus on activities and states, may be an intriguing glimpse into some of what is

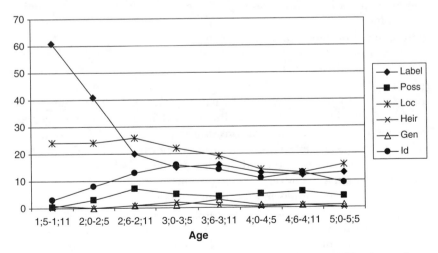

FIGURE 16.—Percentage of label-identity questions over all the children's questions.

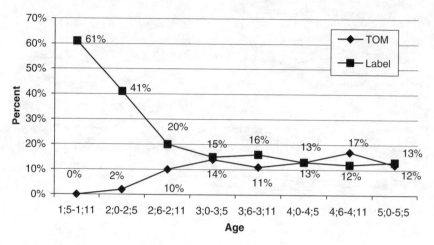

FIGURE 17.—Percentage of combined children's questions that are Theory of Mind (ToM) versus label.

central to the child's thinking about people, animals, and objects during the preschool years.

DISCUSSION

The purpose of Study 1 was to determine to what degree the requirements of the IRM are present during natural, nonspecific interaction between children and their parents. Do children ask questions, particularly questions that ask for information, and are potentially useful for cognitive development? Do parents give informative answers? Do children care about getting the information they ask for?

The results of this study indicate that the majority of questions that children ask seek information. While children can and do ask questions for other purposes—permission, clarification, and so on—the main function of questions for them is to gather information about the world; children are actively engaged in enquiries about the world that surrounds them as they go through their day. These questions sum to an extremely large number of information-seeking questions, on average 76 per hour, when the children are engaged in conversation with adults. Asking questions is not rare or even intermittent for children—it is a constant, natural, central part of their interactions with the adults in their environment.

These adults are very accommodating, and answer the children's questions informatively most of the time. But further, the adults often add additional relevant information beyond what the child requested, information that seems to be helping children to focus on what is important to the topic at hand. So, it is important to note that children's questions do not just get the specific information requested, they open the door for the adults to give whatever information the children need to understand the world and the things in it, even when the children themselves do not know exactly what it is they do not know. This guidance could be helping direct the children's thinking, helping them to determine what is important about a topic at hand, and how they should be thinking about it.

When the adults do fail to answer the questions, children persist in trying to get the information they requested. They are not satisfied simply to get attention from the adult, nor are they just asking questions for the fun of asking them; they keep asking for the information until they receive it, and stop once they do. They do not show this same persistence with other types of conversational turns, and this indicates that questions are privileged in this way; children ask questions when they want input from the adult, and other sorts of utterances are not designed to get an informative response from adults in the way that questions are designed to do so.

Thus, the skills required for the IRM are in place from the earliest age studied here (1;5)—children can, and do, recruit information from others around them who know more about the world and the things in it. This provides them with a wealth of potentially useful information for building up and working out their understandings of the world.

While the basic skills used in the mechanism are present from the earliest age and the so the system does not change with age, the content areas that children apply their questions to changes in ways that reflect the learning process. Both over time and within an exchange, children begin by collecting isolated facts, and then shift more focus toward explanatory questions that relate facts to one another and unify the knowledge structure. This is the same shift seen in adults when they learn about a topic, and move from knowing little about the topic to becoming more expert in it; thus, this shift seems to indicate similar conceptual changes on the part of the children.

Further, the specific content of children's questions, such as questions about labels or ToM, change in ways that parallel the conceptual developments we know them to be making; as they are working out certain puzzles, their questions about these areas of knowledge increase. While the data in this study cannot detect causation between the questions children are asking and the content of their knowledge, this causal relationship will be explored in Chapter V.

The procedure used in Study 1 has a number of strengths. Because data transcription includes everything that was said during the session, every question asked by the children is recorded exactly, along with the exact response they received; thus detailed information about question frequency and response could be carefully calculated. However, these recordings were made in situations that were almost exactly the same during each session, at similar times of day, during similar activities, and represent only a small slice of the child's daily activities. In different situations, the composition of their questions might look completely different; at the least, many low-frequency, high-salience questions that would occur during other situations throughout the day might not be represented, and this may be limiting the data presented in this study.

This study is also limited in the number of subjects included, due to its longitudinal nature. Though this is necessary to allow careful analysis of changes in children's questions as they grow older, and though care was taken to include some diversity in terms of gender, family education, SES, and situational variables, there is very little that can be done with only four children; this limits how far these data can be generalized because what we see in this study may be a product of these four children only. Also, because these were audio recordings, these data cannot include any information about gestures, so they don't tell us anything about preverbal children who are not yet asking linguistic questions but who may use gestural means and vocalizations to ask for information; if recruiting information is an important factor in cognitive development, we'd expect preverbal children to be using some other means available to them to get information. Study 2 used a different methodology to explore children's questions to give a broader picture of these behaviors; though Study 2 has separate goals, it also is designed to complement the methodological particulars of Study 1.

NOTES

3. The use of the word "primary" here is not meant to imply that children are any more emotionally invested in these questions than in other types of questions; getting answer to all types of questions is mostly likely important to children. This term is used simply to indicate that getting information is the most common reason children ask questions.

4. Because there were no explanatory questions in the data set at age 1;5–1;11, this group could not be analyzed, and was not included.

5. Because there were no explanatory questions in the data set at age 1;5–1;11, this group could not be analyzed, and was not included.

6. For ease of comparison over children, each chart contains rows for each age group, even if no data were available for that age. In these cases, the rows are left with empty cells.

III. DIARY STUDY OF CHILDREN'S QUESTIONS

Study 1 tells us a lot about children's question-asking behaviors, but there's more we'd like to know. What about younger children who are not yet asking verbal questions? These children are learning about the world too, and would also benefit from being able to get information from adults when they need it; can they effectively recruit information by "asking" questions via gesture, expressions, and vocalizations? Also, what do children's questions look like in across a broad range of situations? Throughout the day, children may be inside and outside, in cars or planes, may visit people and places; in fact, outside of the home, they are more likely to encounter situations they haven't encountered before. Will the type of questions they ask in these situations have different implications for the possible usefulness of an IRM? Finally, what would we see if we look at a greater number of children? Are the findings seen in Study 1 true only of the four subjects studied? Study 2 looks at these issues.

STUDY 2: METHODS

Participants and Procedure

Sixty-eight children between the ages of 1;0 and 5;0 years participated (for age 1;0–1;5, $n = 13$; for 1;6–1;11, $n = 12$; for 2;0–2;5, $n = 7$; for 2;6–2;11, $n = 7$; for 3;0–3;5, $n = 6$; for 3;6–3;11, $n = 7$; for 4;0–4;5, $n = 8$; for 4;6–4;11, $n = 9$. Note that slightly higher numbers of children were run at the younger ages because data on gestures in younger children was not possible to collect in studies 1 and 3). These children were randomly sampled from the population of Bing Nursery School (BNS), a campus research-oriented preschool, and its waitlist; students in the school and on the waitlist represent the broad demographic characteristics of the San Francisco Bay Area. Because this is a research-oriented preschool, the school makes an effort to bring diversity to the subject population. The ethnic/

45

racial composition of the school is as follows: 2.6% Native American, 24.6% Asian, 10.8% African American, 11.4% Hispanic, and 50.6% White. In addition, BNS has an outreach program designed to bring in children from different SES backgrounds into the school, so that the population is not only made up of middle-class children from educated families; 20% of the student population comes from lower-SES families, and their tuition is paid by scholarship through the outreach program.

During a meeting with the researchers, parents were given forms specially designed to record their children's questions. These forms had space to write down the questions their children asked, what the subject of the question was, whether this was a familiar or unfamiliar subject for the child, any relevant situational information, any response given to the child, and any follow-up questions asked/responses given. The forms were explained to the parents in detail during the initial face-to-face meeting, and researchers called to check-in and follow-up with the parents after data collection began, to make sure everything was clear and that data collection was proceeding as planned. Parents were given multiple recording sets, and were asked both to keep them at hand in a variety of places and to take them along when they went out with their children, so they could record questions as they occurred. Parents recorded questions for one week, and then returned the forms by mail.

In the case of the younger children who were asking nonverbal questions (mostly children aged 1;0–1;5, but also some children aged 1;6–2;0), parents were trained to differentiate and separately record the child's behavior from their interpretation of the behavior, and we stressed the importance of knowing exactly what behaviors children do and do not use to elicit information before they are asking verbal questions. For example, a parent record might report the following: "Situation: I was unpacking groceries. Subject: Kiwi fruit, unfamiliar to the child. Child picked up kiwi, held it toward me with a puzzled expression on her face, and said 'uh?'. This meant 'What is this?'" We trained the parents to separate these out so that we could test the reliability of their judgments; because this procedure includes an interpretation on the part of the parent of the child's behavior, it is important to ensure that parents are making reliable interpretations of their children's behaviors. So, a representative subset of the reported questioning behaviors were coded by eight researchers; these researchers did not know what interpretation the parents had made of the behaviors, and they were not familiar with the coding system used in the study (they were not working on this line of research apart from this one analysis). Ninety-six percent of the time the researchers' interpretation of the behaviors matched the parents' interpretation of those behaviors, indicating the behaviors were reliably interpreted and reported by parents.

Data Analysis

Analysis of this data set uses the same coding system and statistics described for Study 1. Intercoder reliability also proceeded as in Study 1, and again was verified to be at or above 95% reliability for all codes. The target analyses for this data set are as follows:

(1) Do children ask questions, and why?

(2) What general type of information do children ask for?

(3) What specific content to children ask about?

(4) Do adults give additional information to the children?

Note that because this study uses a different methodology and the nature of these data is different, not all of the analyses from Study 1 could be done here. Frequency information is not present here because parents cannot record every question their children ask. Nor is it possible to track the child's persistence, because we have no way of knowing if all repetitions of a question have been recorded. In addition, whether or not a question receives a response may be reported in a biased fashion, as parents are likely biased to record questions they answer and to answer questions they record.

RESULTS

Do Children Ask Questions, and Why?

Table 14 shows the number of questions collected by parents during this study; the total data set contains 4,359 questions, of which 3,533 are information-seeking questions. The first age is of particular importance here;

TABLE 14

NUMBER OF QUESTIONS CONTAINED IN THE DIARY DATA

Age of children (years)	Total questions	Total information-seeking questions
1;–1;5	999	898
1;6–1;11	780	543
2;–2;5	463	332
2;6–2;11	334	235
3;–3;5	352	283
3;6–3;11	487	440
4;–4;5	460	396
4;6–4;11	484	406
Total	4,359	3,533

as predicted, these nonverbal children were just as able as older children to ask for information via gestures, expressions, and vocalizations.

Table 15 breaks the overall data set down by the function of the questions that children ask; here again we see that information-seeking questions are the majority of the questions children ask. This is true at each individual age as well, seen in Figure 18. These data are in line with those reported in study 1; children are here again significantly more likely to use a question to gather information than for other purposes (1;0–1;5, $\chi^2(1) = 64$, $p < .000$; 1;6–1;11, $\chi^2(1) = 16$, $p < .000$; 2;0–2;5, $\chi^2(1) = 19.36$, $p < .000$; 2;5–2;11, $\chi^2(1) = 16$, $p < .000$; 3;0–3;5, $\chi^2(1) = 36$, $p < .000$; 3;6–3;11, $\chi^2(1) = 64$, $p < .000$; 4;0–4;5, $\chi^2(1) = 51.84$, $p < .000$; 4;6–4;11, $\chi^2(1) = 43.56$, $p < .000$). Importantly, this is just as true for children who are not asking verbal questions, but rather are asking questions via gesture and vocalizations; while parents do report that children use these methods to ask for permission and other sorts of questions, overwhelmingly children's questions during this stage are asking for information. So, here again one of the main predictions of Study 2 was borne out—even children who are not yet verbally asking questions are recruiting information effectively from their parents about the world around them.

What General Type of Information Do Children Ask For?

Facts Versus Explanatory Principles

Study 1 found that while the majority of children's questions are asking for facts, as the children get older, their questions are significantly more likely to request explanatory information. Figure 19 shows that the same is

TABLE 15

PERCENT OF EACH QUESTION-TYPE ASKED BY CHILDREN

Question type	%
Information-seeking questions	81
Fact (information-seeking)	67
Explanation (information-seeking)	14
Non-information-seeking questions	19
Attention	1
Clarification	<1
Action	7
Permission	10
Play	<1
Child/animal addressee	<1
Unknown	1

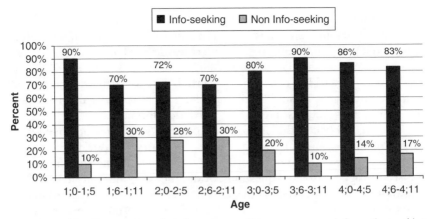

FIGURE 18.—Percentage of information-seeking versus noninformation-seeking questions.

true of the children in Study 2; these children are also significantly more likely to ask for explanatory information as they get older (Pearson's $\chi^2(7) = 77.72, p < .000$). This pattern is not different despite the addition of younger children; the vast majority of questions these younger children ask are asking for facts, despite the fact that even preverbal children have the ability to ask explanatory questions (and 3% of their questions are explanatory questions). So despite a much larger variety of situations reflected in this data set, the pattern does not change; we still see an increase in explanatory questions with age. These data, then, also support the prediction that over the course of the preschool years, children build up a set of facts and shift toward a focus on the explanatory principles that underlie these facts.

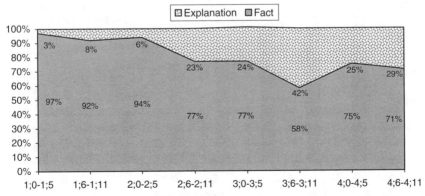

FIGURE 19.—Percentage of questions asking for fact and explanatory information at each age.

In addition, the "A-ha" spike in explanatory questions seen in Study 1 for each of the four children is seen here; despite the cross-sectional nature of these data, the same spike occurs with children aged 3;6–3;11 (3;0–3;5 vs. 3;6–3;11, Pearson's $\chi^2(1) = 7.58$, $p < .006$; 3;6–3;11 vs. 4;0–4;5, Pearson's $\chi^2(1) = 6.49$, $p < .011$). Thus, this pattern is not an artifact of the small number of subjects in study one, but seems to reflect a real spike in explanatory interest at this stage of cognitive development.

The second half of the prediction is that this shift from fact to explanatory principles will occur not just over the course of development, but within a given exchange on a particular topic, as well. Did the children in this study ask only isolated questions, or did they ask questions that built on one another within a series of questions? By asking parents to record follow-up questions on the same sheet as the original question, we allowed for analysis of this issue. Figure 20 shows that from the earliest age when children ask questions via nonlinguistic methods, children do ask questions that build on one another, and as the children get older, building questions increase significantly and become roughly half of the questions that children ask (Pearson's $\chi^2(7) = 141.196$, $p < .000$). At every age, the proportion of questions that build on previous questions is lower than seen in Study 1; this is likely due to the fact that it is very demanding for parents to write down every question a child asks, while multiple questions are easily captured when taping conversations. Importantly, despite these differences, the direction is preserved here, and so the overall finding remains.

Are the children more likely to ask for explanatory information later in a building exchange than they are when asking an isolated question or the first question in a building exchange? Figure 21 shows that with only one exception, it is significantly more likely that a building question will be an explanatory question than the first question of an exchange (1;0–1;5,

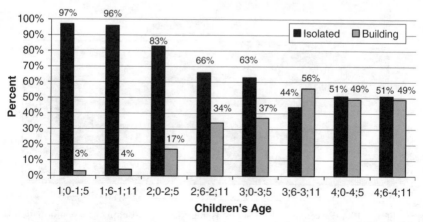

FIGURE 20.—Percentage of questions that are isolated versus building.

50

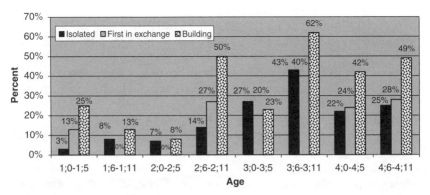

FIGURE 21.—Percentage of explanatory questions in isolated versus building questions.

$\chi^2(1) = 3.79, p < .05$; 1;6–1;11, $\chi^2(1) = 10.29, p < .001$; 2;0–2;5, $\chi^2(1) = 5.44$, $p < .02$; 2;6–2;11, $\chi^2(1) = 6.87, p < .009$; 3;6–3;11, $\chi^2(1) = 4.75, p < .029$; 4;0–4;5, $\chi^2(1) = 4.91, p < .027$; 4;6–4;11, $\chi^2(1) = 5.73, p < .017$); the exception is age 3;0–3;5, when it is equally likely ($\chi^2(1) = .209, p < .647$). Here again, then, we see the shift from fact to explanatory questions within building exchanges.

Also, in the majority of cases, a question is significantly more likely to be an explanatory question when it is a building question than when it is an isolated question (1;0–1;5, $\chi^2(1) = 17.29$; 2;6–2;11, $\chi^2(1) = 20.25, p < .000$; 3;6–3;11, $\chi^2(1) = 3.44, p = <.06$, trend approaching significance; 4;0–4;5, $\chi^2(1) = 6.25, p < .012$; 4;6–4;11, $\chi^2(1) = 7.78, p < .005$), and in the remaining cases, it is equally likely, but not less likely (1;6–1;11, $\chi^2(1) = 1.19, p < .28$; 2;0–2;5, $\chi^2(1) = .067, p < .796$; 3;0–3;5, $\chi^2(1) = .320, p < .572$).

An important difference from study one is that one of these findings does show a change with age. While the likelihood that the first question in an exchange vs. a building question is an explanatory question remains the same over all the age groups (Pearson's $\chi^2(7) = 10.07, p = .185$), it becomes more likely that a building question will be an explanatory question than will an isolated question as the child gets older (Pearson's $\chi^2(7) = 22.58$, $p < .002$). This increase may be due to the smaller number of building questions compared to isolated questions found in the younger ages to start out with, as well as the younger initial age group.

What Content Do Children Ask About?

One of the possible problems with Study 1 is that the specific content of children's questions may be an artifact of the restricted situations the children were in; they interacted with largely the same items and activities, always within the home, almost always at the same time of day. It's possible, then, that the questions children asked were tied to that context, and are not representative of the questions children ask across a broader range of situations. Also, it's possible that the small number of subjects artificially influenced the results reported in Study 1. So, one of the primary goals of Study 2 is to collect a data set of the questions that children ask in a larger set of situational contexts.

Table 16 reports the contents of the questions asked by the children in Study 2. Despite the fact that children were in a much wider variety of situations (indoors, outdoors, in cars, at museums, etc.), the types of things that interested the children remained the same. Here again for the children, appearance, property, part, count, possession, hierarchy, and generalization questions were infrequent, and remained relatively stable over time. Questions about function, activities, theory of mind (ToM), state and identity were a larger proportion of the child's questions, and increased over time to varying degrees. And again questions asking for labels started out comprising a large percentage of the children's questions, and decreased over time; this is even more true here of labels, which comprise 94% of the youngest age group, a group that goes 6 months younger than Study 1. This high percentage of labels also further strengthens the possibility that children start off asking more for facts and are trying to sort categories out before moving on to fleshing those categories out with further information and explanatory principles.

To highlight once again the trends found with respect to label questions and ToM questions, Figure 22 shows that questions asking for labels are a higher percentage when the children are younger, at the time we know them to be more concerned with learning object categories, and this decreases as the children get older (Pearson's $\chi^2(7) = 192.06$, $p < .000$). And again, ToM questions are increasing as children get older, at times when we know children to be making more advances in ToM (Pearson's $\chi^2(7) = 18.16$, $p < .011$).

What about the younger, preverbal children included in this study? If the patterns found in Study 1 were not artifacts of the limited situations and small number of children involved in that study, we'd predict that if we looked at younger children, based on the trends in Study 1, we'd see these children asking even more questions about labels and even fewer questions about theory of mind. Figure 3.5 shows that this is exactly what we find. This is further evidence that the specific content of the questions found in both of these studies point to real trends in children's interest as they move through cognitive development.

Do Adults Give Additional Information to the Children?

Finally, while it is not possible to perform the response analyses done in Study 1, because parents are biased towards recording questions that they

52

TABLE 16

PERCENT OF EACH QUESTION TYPE IN CHILDREN'S QUESTIONS

	Appearance	Property	Part	Function	Activities	Theory of Mind	State	Count	Label	Possession	Loc	Heirarchy	Generalization	Identity
1;0–1;5	0	1	3	2	1	0	1	0	94	0	1	0	0.1	2
1;6–1;11	0	1	5	1	7	4	5	2	68	1	12	1	0.2	10
2;0–2;5	0	2	4	5	17	4	3	0.3	31	2	30	1	3	22
2;6–2;11	2	6	2	6	34	9	13	0	17	2	27	1	0.4	11
3;0–3;5	1	7	2	9	39	14	11	2	14	5	36	0.3	9	12
3;6–3;11	2	11	2	8	34	4	20	2	10	9	13	1	9	14
4;0–4;5	2	10	5	11	34	6	17	3	14	3	17	1	10	11
4;6–4;11	3	6	2	9	23	8	18	5	24	5	8	1	3	16

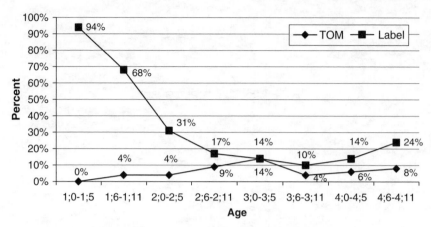

FIGURE 22.—Percentage of ToM versus Label questions.

answered (and towards answering questions that they record!), it is possible to examine the amount of additional information that parents give to their children when they answer them. Figure 23 shows that just as in the CHILDES data, parents are giving additional information to their children, particularly to the youngest groups of children who may not know what specific information they need to understand the topic at hand (Pearson's $\chi^2(7) = 27.56$, $p < .000$). Particularly interesting is the first age group, as it contains only children who are eliciting information via gesture and non-word verbalizations; parents seem particularly helpful here when it comes to giving children extra information about the things that have captured their attention. These questioning gestures, expressions, and vocalizations also open the door for parents to help guide the children's thinking about the world around them, at a time when the child is paying particular attention.

Are these parents giving additional information differentially depending on the type of question? Figure 24 shows again that question type does

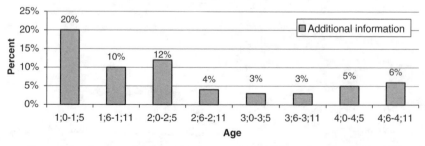

FIGURE 23.—Percent of informative responses to children that contained additional information.

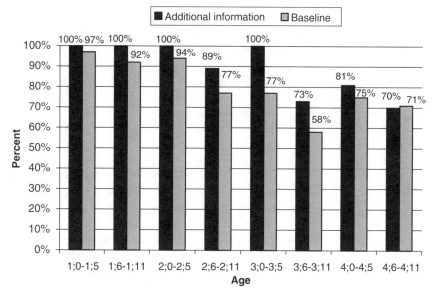

FIGURE 24.—Percentage of questions receiving additional information that ask for facts at each age.

not determine whether or not the parent gives additional information to the child; parents give additional information at rates that do not differ from the baseline occurrence of these question types (1;0–1;5, $\chi^2(1) = .046$, $p = .831$; 1;6–1;11, $\chi^2(1) = .333$, $p = .564$; 2;0–2;5, $\chi^2(1) = .186$, $p = .667$; 2;6–2;11, $\chi^2(1) = .867$, $p < .352$; 3;0–3;5, $\chi^2(1) = 2.989$, $p = .084$; 3;6–3;11, $\chi^2(1) = 1.718$, $p = .190$; 4;0–4;5, $\chi^2(1) = .231$, $p = .631$; 4;6–4;11, $\chi^2(1) = .007$, $p < .933$). Here again the situation and not the question type seems to determine when additional information is given.

DISCUSSION

Study 2 looked to build on Study 1 by investigating how younger children who cannot yet ask linguistic questions might be able to recruit information by other means; it also built on those findings by looking at a larger range of situations and a larger number of subjects.

Despite large methodological differences and a much larger number of children, the findings of Study 2 again show that the basic skills required for the IRM are present from the earliest age studied, age 1;0–1;5. At this age, children are not yet asking linguistic questions, but ask questions via gesture and vocalizations; these methods are just as efficient at recruiting information from the parents as are linguistic questions, and may be help-ing children learn from very early on in their development. In fact, parents seem to be even more likely to give pre-verbal children extra information relevant to their questions; these "questions" create opportunities that allow parents to guide their children's thinking from very early on. Even within this young group of pre-verbal children, the vast majority of children's questions are still seeking information, and this continues on again as the children get older, suggesting that children are using questions to learn about the world from the start.

While the skills are present from the start, the content that the mech-anism is applied to changes as the children get older and their needs shift. As in Study 1, children's questions are primarily asking for facts, a finding that remains the same with the preverbal children, but in the older age groups, more and more of the children's questions ask for explanatory information. This also holds within a particular exchange; children ask both isolated questions and questions that occur in a series that build on one another, and it is the building questions that are more likely to shift from fact questions to more explanatory information. So, the shift predicted by the adult literature is again found here, a shift that in adults goes along with greater expertise in a given area.

Further, despite a much wider variety of situations, the specific content of information that children ask for remains the same as that reported in Study 1. The findings here are not limited to one situation only, and so the proportions of questions we see asking about a given type of information seem to be a reflection not of a given situation or type of object, but of how much certain aspects of the world are of intrinsic interest to the children at a given point in their development. The younger, preverbal children add to these data in an important way; the patterns are buttressed by the data from these children, with the youngest children asking even more questions about labels (for example), and asking even fewer questions about ToM. This addition again fits with the direction we know children's cognitive development to be taking at these ages.

In addition to providing data about preverbal children's question-asking abilities, and additional support of other hypotheses at hand, Study 2 also works with Study 1 to validate the findings presented by both studies. Whereas Study 1 is a longitudinal study that takes place in a limited set of situations, Study 2 is a cross-sectional study that gathers questions over a wide variety of circumstances. Although Study 1 presents veridical information that includes detailed information on every question and answer within the target period, it misses low-frequency, high-salience items; however, Study 2 captures these items, making it less likely that something important is being missed. And the veridical data collected in Study 1 don't have these problemss. Despite these large differences in methodology, both studies report the same findings and support the hypotheses; thus, this greatly decreases any likelihood that the results are a function of the particular children involved in a study (an important concern in the CHILDES data, which consists of data from only four children) or are limited to a particular situation (because the diary data span a large variety of situations). We can be confident that the patterns reported here are tapping into something real.

While both of these studies give a sense of what the child's interests are generally, over a broad range of subjects, neither of them is able to closely investigate the questions that children ask within a single domain. Study 3 looks to examine the questions children ask about one specific set of stimulus items and one specific domain: animals and naïve biology.

IV. CHILDREN'S QUESTIONS ABOUT ANIMALS

Do the questions children ask within a single domain have the potential to help them learn about that domain? Study 3 investigates this issue by looking at the questions asked about one specific topic, animals, and a potentially corresponding domain of knowledge, naïve biology. Studies 1 and 2 are both, to a degree, subject to the whims of fate—the questions the children ask will likely vary from child to child depending on the particular situation they are in, or the particular objects they are faced with; no two children can be counted on to ask a question on the same topic. While Study 1 was more limited in situation than Study 2, there is still a wide variety of items that the children are asking about in both studies—food, household objects, toys, people, items in purses, and so on. Because of this wide variety of different objects, the content of the questions children ask reflects the overall experience of their exploration throughout the day, and does not yield enough data about any one domain for further analysis. So, these studies do not allow us to investigate any one area to see how such questions could be potentially related to advances in related domains of knowledge. To investigate these issues, Study 3 gathers a large number of questions related to animals via a cross-sectional, veridical corpus of questions collected in a controlled set of situations where animals are the children's primary focus, and examines their relation to developments in the domain of naïve biology.

ANIMALS AND BIOLOGICAL KNOWLEDGE

Research that examines the development of children's thinking about biological phenomena suggests that many big changes take place in their understanding of this domain between the ages of 4–10. Work by Carey (1985) suggests that children undergo important shifts in their causal understandings of biological phenomena beginning around, and after, the age of 4; Carey argues that children shift from a psychological causal understanding of biological phenomena to a vitalistic causal understanding during these years, and that their concepts of living things change in accord with this shift. Jaaokola and Slaughter (2002) argue that between the ages of 4 and 6, children undergo a reorganization of their understanding of the function of the body, and this corresponds to the discovery of the maintenance of the life cycle as an important goal of biological functioning. In addition, children's understanding of death seems to change substantially after the age of 4; Kenyon (2001) reviewed the literature in this area and summarizes it as finding that 4-year-olds have some understanding of death, but that it is very incomplete and that knowledge improves gradually until the age of 10.

Further, Johnson and Solomon (1997) and Solomon et al. (1996) find that children show a gradual increase in the understanding of biological principles of inheritance between the ages of 4–5 years of age and 6–7 years of age; similarly, Springer and Keil (1989) found that 4- and 5-year-olds (studied as a group) were less likely to understand these principles than 6- and 7-year-olds, and Solomon (2002) found that 4-year-olds are not any more likely to say that a child resembles a biological parent than an adoptive parent, while 5-year-olds are more likely to say the child will resemble a biological parent. With respect to germs and illness, Siegal (1988) found that 4- and 5-year-olds (studied as a group) had an incomplete understanding of contagion, and that this understanding improved over time, with first- and third-graders showing an improved understanding of these issues; similarly, Solomon and Cassimatis (1999) found that preschoolers did not understand the role that germs play in illness, and why people get sick. Finally, children also make advances after the age of 4 with respect to understanding growth as a biological process; Rosengren (1991) found that it is not until age 5 that children understand that animals get bigger and not smaller with age, and that younger children failed to understand the nature of changes in size. Younger children did not expect changes in appearance to go along with changes in size; when asked to choose an appropriate example of a grown animal, they were just as likely to choose a large animal that resembled a baby as to choose a large animal that differed in color and shape, while older children and adults chose the large animal that differed in color and shape.

If children's understanding of the domain of biology, particularly their causal understanding, is going to be shifting after the age of 4, the model presented in this paper predicts that starting just before this age, we'd see an increase in questions about the domain of biology, particularly in the explanatory questions that they ask about biological phenomena. According to this model, when children encounter something they do not understand, asking a question recruits information that then allows the corresponding knowledge state to be revised toward a more adult-like state; this may occur with single questions, but also over more than one questioning episode over time. So, we would expect questions to begin before and along with the relevant shifts reported in the above literature; we'd expect children to be trying to work out these puzzles just before this age, and be asking questions about these phenomena that help them do that. Accordingly, the data gathered in this study allow us to examine the questions children ask about animals, and how many of these questions target biological information (vs., e.g., the surface appearance of the animals), before and at the age of 4 years.

STIMULUS TYPE

Also, in Studies 1 and 2, different sorts of stimulus items were lumped together in the analyses, and were difficult to pull apart—children engaged with real objects, pictures of objects, and toy replicas of objects. But children's experience of real objects versus representations of objects may have important consequences for how they engage with these objects and learn from them. Much of the work that is done on children's understanding of biological phenomena is done with drawings or pictures of the target animals or people; in much of this literature, there is an implicit assumption that such stimuli are an adequate stand-in for real animals. However, information that is relevant to biological phenomena is possibly being lost in these stimuli; because of this, children may show different types of engagement in these different stimuli. If this is so, children may be less likely to ask questions about biological phenomena when engaged with these stimuli. Study 3 examines how children's questions change in these different instances by varying the type of stimuli children interact with.

GENERAL QUESTIONS ANALYSIS

Finally, because the sessions in Study 3 were recorded and transcribed verbatim, this study allows us to validate all of the analyses performed in Study 1, including those done on frequency information, response information, information on the children's persistence, and so on (not possible with Study 2), while the cross-sectional nature of the data eliminates the problems with individual differences associated with having only four subjects in the CHILDES study.

To summarize, this study has three general goals:

> (1) To investigate questions that are specific to the domain of biological knowledge.

(2) To investigate how stimulus type impacts the questions that children ask about the domain of biological knowledge.

(3) To validate the findings reported in Studies 1 and 2.

Specific hypotheses are outlined below.

STUDY 3: HYPOTHESES

General Questions Analyses

First, there is no reason to believe that the basic functioning of the Information-Requesting Mechanism would be different when applied to a specific area of cognitive development; therefore, we would predict that the overall rates of information-seeking questions, response rate, rate of persistence, and general question type (fact, explanatory) would be the same as those found in Studies 1 and 2.

Second, while the same general content information is likely to interest children across domains, there are some areas within the content codes that we would predict will vary due to the specific situation. The following differences are predicted:

(1) Because many of the animals in this study are novel to children this age, we might expect to see more questions asking for labels, particularly in older children (who showed a drop-off in label questions in Studies 1 and 2); we would expect that even older children would still be asking what some of the animals are called.

(2) If children's knowledge of other's minds is limited to people at this age, we would expect to see fewer questions asking about Theory of Mind (ToM) than we saw in their questions during Studies 1 and 2; if children believe that animals also have minds, we would expect to see no difference in the frequency of questions about ToM.

(3) Because animals are likely to move around, the code "activity," used in the schema used for Studies 1 and 2, could be expected to apply more to biological creatures. So, we would predict that children would be more likely to ask about activities in this study.

Animals and Biological Knowledge

Third, if children are working out the domain of biology, we would expect to see more questions regarding biological phenomena when children are focused on animals than in other situations. There are two important points to note about this prediction. First, while it logically follows that children will be asking more questions about animals when in a zoo situation, note that it does not necessarily follow logically that these questions about animals will target biological phenomena. Children could simply ask questions about the nonbiological aspects of the animals, such as labels, appearance, parts, environments, and so on, just as when they are dealing with objects that are not animals. However, an increase in questions that are specific to biological phenomena (maintenance of life, causes of death, growth, principles of inheritance) would be an indication that the child is attempting to gather information about the domain of biology specifically, rather than other sorts of information about animals, and thus would indicate that they are trying to work out this causal domain.

The second important point to make about this prediction is that it is not claiming that children are not interested in biology in other situations such as those examined in Studies 1 and 2. There are two possibilities here; one is that children are in fact less interested in biological information in such situations, and the second possibility is that their interest in biology is simply masked in those situations by their interest in the other types of objects that are present. The prediction here argues for the second possibility, that children *are* interested in biological knowledge as they draw closer to age 4, but we cannot examine this adequately in the previous studies because the situations in those studies mask this interest. So, Study 3 presents stimulus materials focused in this domain, so we can test for any interest in biological phenomena.

Also, because children at the ages studied here are on the verge of beginning to make conceptual shifts with respect to biological phenomena, and because these shifts seem to revolve around the explanatory/core principles in this domain as reviewed above, we would expect to see an increase in explanatory questions as children move toward the age of 4 and at the age of 4, over and above the level of explanatory questions about other phenomena in general.

As the coding schema used for Studies 1 and 2 did not specifically target this type of information, a separate analysis was conducted on both the current data and a comparison sample taken from the data in Study 1; this is described below.

Stimulus Type

Finally, if there is a difference in how children are engaged by real animals versus drawings or three-dimensional replicas of animals due to the more impoverished nature of these stimuli, we predict they will ask fewer questions and fewer causal questions about biological phenomena when engaged with drawings or replicas.

METHODS

Participants and Procedure

One hundred and twelve children between the ages of 2;0–2;9 ($n = 36$; mean age 2;3.5), 3;0–3;9 ($n = 41$; mean age 3;4), and 4;0–4;9 ($n = 35$; mean age 4;5) participated. Participants were drawn from the population of Bing Nursery School, a campus research-oriented preschool. Parent–child dyads were equipped with wireless microphones, and walked through one of three zoos: (1) a small local children's zoo with live animals, (2) a small zoo created using three-dimensional toy replicas of those same animals, (3) a small zoo created using line drawings of those same animals. The animals were a combination of familiar (e.g., ducks, fish, turtles) and unfamiliar animals (e.g., bobcat, skink, guinea fowl, ferrets). In order to make the drawings more representative of the activities the animals engaged in at the real zoo, approximately half of the drawings depicted the animals engaged in a variety of activities (e.g., eating, sleeping, walking, jumping)—this is, at a minimum, the same number of animals any given child observed engaged in an activity in the real animal zoo (in some cases, more). While it was not possible to have the three dimensional replicas of animals engaged in activities, it is still possible for children to attribute activities to them because of their pose (e.g., sleeping, sitting, swimming, walking); in addition, the more realistic colors and shapes of the animal replicas give children rich information that may tap into deeper conceptual knowledge than do drawings of animals.

Each parent–child pair visited only one of the three zoos, and proceeded through their zoo viewing exhibits in a counterbalanced order. An audio recording was made of the conversation between parent and child, and these recordings were transcribed for data analysis. The full recording was transcribed, from the moment the parent/child dyad entered the zoo, to the moment they came back out to where the experimenter was waiting.

Data Analysis

(1) *General question analyses*: All of the questions asked by the children were coded according to same system and statistics used for Studies 1 and 2.

(2) *Biological knowledge analyses*: An additional analysis was performed, targeting questions asking about biological information. If children are starting to build up an understanding of the domain of naïve biology at this

age, we would expect that they would ask more biologically specific questions than at other ages and in other situations. If they are not building up this understanding yet, we would not expect to see more questions about biological phenomena; instead, we would expect that children's questions about animals would be asking for information about labels, appearance, parts, and so on, with no increase in questions about biological phenomena. So, we would expect to see more questions about targeted biological information in the zoo data than in other situations, due to the focused nature of these stimuli; we'd expect to see quantitatively more of these questions here. Note that in both Studies 1 and 2, children were always around people, who are biological entities and who would be expected to draw biologically specific questions; they were sometimes around pets, as well. So, some biologically related questions would be expected in these circumstances, just not as many as in the zoo data.

The primary analysis investigating this hypothesis used the data gathered in the real animal condition of this study, and compared these data to a sample taken from the CHILDES data gathered in Study 1. For the CHILDES data, 200 information-seeking questions were taken at random corresponding to each of the age groups present in the zoo data, 2;0–2;9, 3;0–3;9 and 4;0–4;9. All information-seeking questions were coded as either asking for biological information, or nonbiological information. The definition of biological information used in this analysis included questions that asked about biologically necessary processes such as those in the literature reviewed above. These include processes that are required to maintain life (sleeping, eating, drinking, defecating, etc.), processes related to biological inheritance (reproduction, etc.), processes related to growth and transformations, and processes that are directly asking about the life cycle, illness, and death. Examples of such questions were "Why is he sleeping?", "Is he dead?", "Why did he die?", "How do bees grow their babies?", "What do bats like to eat?", "Then they grow a new skin?" (asking about a snake that had shed his skin), "[They eat their vegetables] so they can grow?" Any other questions were coded as nonbiological questions; examples include questions asking for labels ("What's its name?"), properties ("Is the iguana soft?"), positional information ("Why is he up in the tree?"), parts ("Where is his head?"), and so on. Questions were tabulated and chi-square analyses were used to test significant differences.

(3) *Stimulus type analyses*: Secondary analyses compared the data from the real animal condition to the data from the drawing and replica conditions of the current study, to investigate the hypothesis that stimulus type has an effect on how children engage with and learn from different materials. Again questions were tabulated and chi-square analyses were used to test significant differences.

TABLE 17

NUMBER OF ALL QUESTIONS ASKED BY THE CHILDREN DURING TRANSCRIPTION

Age	Total Questions	Total Length of Corpus (Hours)	Questions Per Hour
2;0–2;9	571	6.06	94
3;0–3;9	1122	7.36	152
4;0–4;9	795	6.29	126
Total	2488	19.71	126

RESULTS

Do Children Ask Questions, and Why?

Table 17 shows the number of questions asked by the children during their zoo visits. A total of 2,488 questions were asked during approximately 20 hours of recorded conversation (real animal condition: 13.28 hours, average length of tape = 22.23 minutes; picture condition: 3.25 hours, average length of tape = 4.87 minutes; replica condition 3.18 hours, average length of tape = 5.30 minutes). This averages out to 126 questions per hour.

What percentage of these questions asked for information? As shown in Figure 25, between 73% and 78% of these questions are asking for information; these levels align with the data found in Studies 1 and 2. Here again the primary purpose of children's question-asking behavior is to gather information about the world, because these levels are significantly higher than the percentages of questions used for other purposes (2;0–2;9: $\chi^2(1) = 23.04$, $p < .000$; 3;0–3;9: $\chi^2(1) = 31.36$, $p < .000$; 4;0–4;9:

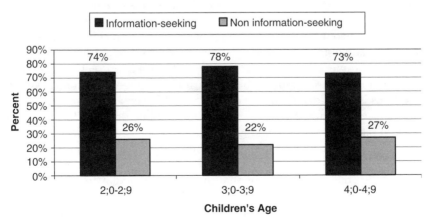

FIGURE 25.—Percentage of information-seeking and noninformation-seeking questions at each age.

TABLE 18

NUMBER OF INFORMATION-SEEKING QUESTIONS ASKED BY CHILDREN DURING SESSIONS

Age	Total Information-Seeking Questions	Total Length of Corpus (Hours)	Questions Per Hour
2;0–2;9	420	6.06	69
3;0–3;9	879	7.36	119
4;0–4;9	580	6.29	92
Total	1,879	19.71	95

$\chi^2(1) = 21.16$, $p < .001$). This again does not change with age (Pearson's $\chi^2(2) = .747$, $p = .688$).

How do these percentages add up in terms of the numbers of information-seeking questions that children ask? Table 18 shows the total number of information-seeking questions asked by children during the transcription; children asked 1,879 questions over the course of the 20 hours of recorded conversation, averaging out to 95 questions per hour, over three questions every 2 minutes. So, the high frequency of information-seeking questions found in Study 1 is confirmed here; in fact, the frequency is even higher in these data. This is most likely due to the focused one-on-one nature of these interactions; during this task, parent and child are mutually engaged in a joint-attention task, while in the CHILDES transcripts, parents and children were sometimes engaged in nonshared activities. A second possibility is that children ask more questions here because they are dealing with a domain that is currently of particular interest to them; a third possibility is that, because there were a number of unfamiliar animals in the zoo, children had more questions than they would have had on average through their day with familiar objects. Whichever the reason, these data suggest that the numbers found in Study 1 were not extreme, but might even underestimate the frequencies of information-seeking questions that occur in some situations. These data again highlight how central asking questions is to children's daily experience—children are constantly asking questions, constantly gathering information about the world. This is an integral part of their interactions with other people.

Were parents in this study as accommodating as those in Study 1? Figure 26 shows that they were; parents were significantly more likely to answer the children's questions than not, at rates similar to those seen in study 1 (2;0–2;9: $\chi^2(1) = 31.36$, $p < .000$; 3;0–3;9: $\chi^2(1) = 46.24$, $p < .000$); 4;0–4;9: $\chi^2(1) = 51.84$, $p = .000$). The likelihood that parents will answer the questions does not change with age (Pearson's $\chi^2(2) = 2.419$, $p = .298$). This is further evidence that the mechanism is in place from early on—here

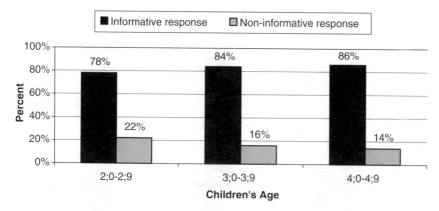

FIGURE 26.—Percentage of children's questions eventually given informative answers.

again even the youngest children studied are effectively gathering information from parents by asking questions.

These parents also give additional help. Figure 27 shows that parents' informational answers are not limited to only the information children ask for; in many cases, parents add additional information that helps children along the road to understanding the topic at hand. This again happens more often the younger the children are, dropping off as the children get older (Pearson's $\chi^2(2) = 9.524, p < .009$). Parents are being even more helpful when children are younger and know less about the world.

Are parents in this study giving this additional information differentially according to question type? The baseline information for how many questions of each sort the children ask will be seen in Figure 30. Figure 28 shows the percent of fact questions that received additional information versus the baseline number of fact questions asked by the children. Here again, parents do not offer additional information more for one question

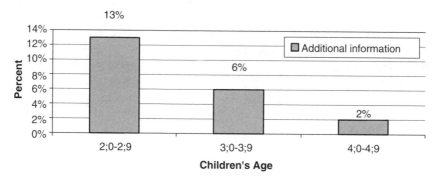

FIGURE 27.—Percentage of informative responses to children's questions that contain additional information.

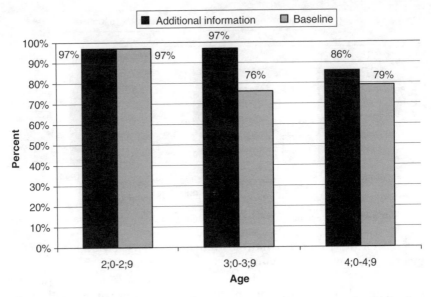

FIGURE 28.—Percentage of questions receiving additional information that ask for facts at each age.

type than the other (2;0–2;9: $\chi^2(1) = .000$, $p = 1$; 3;0–3;9: $\chi^2(1) = 2.549$, $p = .110$); 4;0–4;9: $\chi^2(1) = .297$, $p = .586$).

How Persistent Are Children at Getting the Information They Are Requesting?

What happens in the rare cases when children do not get the information they ask for? As previously discussed, children may simply be repeating their questions to get attention, or simply because they enjoy asking questions. What happens when they get a response (and, therefore, the parent's attention), but the response does not contain the information they requested? Figure 29 shows that children in this study are also are much more likely to repeat the question when they get a response that does not contain the target information than when they get a response that does contain the target information (2;0–2;9: $\chi^2(1) = .44.643$, $p < .000$; 3;0–3;9: $\chi^2(1) = 38.72$, $p < .000$; 4;0–4;9: $\chi^2(1) = 51.271$, $p < .000$); in both cases they are getting attention, but it is only when they receive the target information that they stop asking the question. This does not change with age (Pearson's $\chi^2(2) = .447$, $p = .800$).

What General Type of Information Do Children Ask for?

As previously discussed, based on research done in the adult literature, if children are building up information about a concept/category/domain,

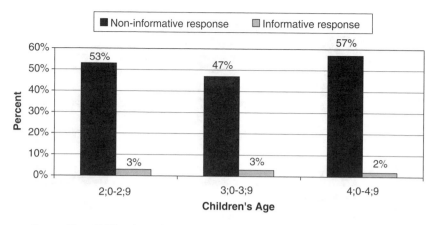

FIGURE 29.—Children's persistence after noninformative responses versus informative responses.

we would expect children to first build up a store of facts about a topic, and then switch to a greater focus on explanatory causal principles that underlie that topic. We would expect to see this both over time as children build richer conceptual structures, and within a given exchange about an item, if the children ask more than one question. Figure 30 shows what happens over the course of development; at all times, fact questions are the majority of the questions asked by children, but as the children get older, there is a significant increase in the number of explanatory questions they ask (Pearson's $\chi^2(2) = 19.196$, $p < .000$). The overall rates of these questions at each age are very similar to the rates found in Studies 1 and 2. So, here again

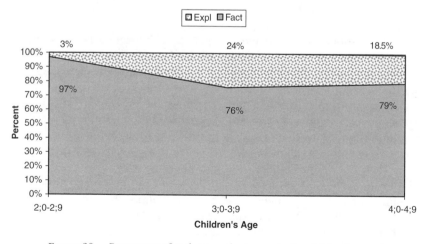

FIGURE 30.—Percentage of each general category in the children's questions.

69

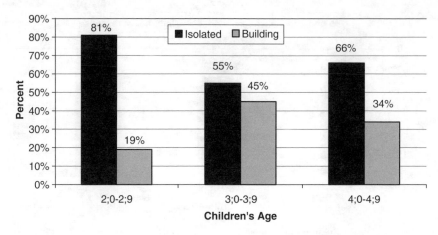

FIGURE 31.—Percentage of the children's questions that are isolated versus building.

children seem to be building up a set of facts, and then relating those facts more and more through deeper explanatory core principles. We also see a trend toward the "A-ha" spike found in Studies 1 and 2, occurring at around age 3;0–3;9 in these data; while this spike is significantly higher than the rate of explanatory questions at age 2;0–2;9 (2;0–2;9 vs. 3;0–3;9: Pearson's $\chi^2(1) = 18.882$, $p < .000$), it is not significantly higher than the rate of these questions at age 4;0–4;9 (3;0–3;9 vs. 4;0–4;9: Pearson's $\chi^2(1) = .258$, $p = .611$). This failure to reach significance may be due to the larger age groupings in these data as compared to the other studies; nonetheless, despite the less finely graded detail of these data, the largest increase in explanatory questions in these data occur between ages 2;0–2;9 and 3;0–3;9, and then drop off between ages 3;0–3;9 and 4;0–4;9, the same pattern seen in the previous studies.

What happens within an exchange? When children ask more than one question about a topic, do they first ask for facts, and then switch focus to explanatory information? Did the children in this study even ask series of questions about a topic as found in previous studies, or do they simply ask single questions in isolation? Figure 31 shows the percentage of children's exchanges on a topic that consisted of either isolated questions, or a series of continuous questions that asked about the same topic. While isolated questions are common at all ages, children have many exchanges that contain more than one question about a topic. These start at approximately one-fifth of the child's questions occurring in series of questions that build on one another, and rise to between one-third to almost half of the questions they ask, numbers in line with the data seen in Studies 1 and 2.

Is there a tendency within these building exchanges to ask more for explanatory questions as the children ask more questions? Figure 32 shows

70

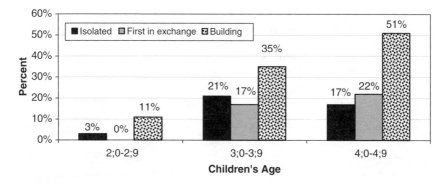

FIGURE 32.—Percentage of the children's isolated versus building questions that are explanatory questions.

the percentage of questions that are asking for explanatory information when the question is an isolated question, the first question in an exchange, or a question that occurs later in a building exchange. This figure shows that a question is significantly more likely to be asking for explanatory information if it is a question occurring later in a building exchange than if it is the first question in a building exchange (2;0–2;9: $\chi^2(1) = 8.333$, $p < .004$; 3;0–3;9: $\chi^2(1) = 6.231$, $p < .013$; 4;0–4;9: $\chi^2(1) = 11.521$, $p < .001$), or if it is an isolated question (2;0–2;9: $\chi^2(1) = 4.571$, $p < .033$; 3;0–3;9: $\chi^2(1) = 3.5$, $p < .061$ [trend approaching significance]; 4;0–4;9: $\chi^2(1) = 17$, $p < .000$). There is no difference in this likelihood if the question is an isolated question versus the first question in an exchange (2;0–2;9: $\chi^2(1) = 1$, $p = .317$; 3;0–3;9: $\chi^2(1) = .421$, $p = .516$; 4;0–4;9: $\chi^2(1) = .641$, $p = .423$), which indicates that isolated questions and first questions play a similar role in the child's thinking, with further questions elaborating on the initial query. So, the children in this study also seem to be first building up a store of facts about the topic at hand, and then switching to a greater emphasis on explanatory information that relates those facts, even within a single exchange on a topic. This does not change with age (isolated vs. building: Pearson's $\chi^2(2) = 2.809$, $p = .245$; first vs. building: Pearson's $\chi^2(2) = 2.865$, $p = .239$; isolated vs. first: Pearson's $\chi^2(2) = 2.050$, $p = .359$); here again, the mechanism is in place from the start.

What Content Do Children Ask About?

What was the specific content of the questions children asked when discussing animals? The overall contents of the questions children asked in this study are presented in Table 19. Three predictions were made about how these data might be different than the data seen in previous studies, because this study focuses on animals. Did children show less of a drop-off in

71

TABLE 19

	Appropriate (%)	Property (%)	Part (%)	Function (%)	Activity (%)	Theory of Mind (%)	State (%)
2;0–2;10	>1	>1	1	7	10	5	2
3;0–3;10	1	4	2	7	19	5	8
4;0–4;10	3	4	1	9	19	9	7

	Count (%)	Label (%)	Possession (%)	Location (%)	Hierarchy (%)	General-ization (%)	Identity (%)
2;0–2;10	1	45	2	26	1	6	8
3;0–3;10	1	30	4	25	2	5	9
4;0–4;10	3	33	2	16	2	7	12

questions asking about labels, because many of the animals were novel to them? Did they ask more about activities? Did they ask fewer ToM questions? As indicated above, the primary analyses here use the data from the real animal condition of the zoo data and a representative sample of the CHILDES data from Study 1.

The prediction that children would ask more questions about labels, given the high number of novel animals in the zoo, was borne out, as seen in Table 19 and Figure 33. The number of questions asking for labels did not decrease as steeply as in the CHILDES and diary studies; the age trend in this case is not significant (Pearson's $\chi^2(2) = 5.469$, $p = .065$), where it was significant in those studies. This reflects a greater number of questions about labels asked between the ages of 4;0 and 4;9 than in the previous studies; while children this age in this study asked for labels 33% of the time, children this age asked for labels in 12% of their questions in Study 1, and 19% of their questions in Study 2.

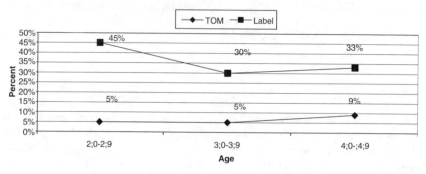

FIGURE 33.—Percentage of children's questions that are ToM versus label.

The second prediction argues that if children do not think of animals as having minds, we would see fewer ToM questions in this study than in the other studies, and that if they do consider animals to be appropriate candidates for things that have minds, we would not see a decrease in ToM questions. Table 19 and Figure 33 show that we see an increase in ToM questions as the children get older in this study, just as in the previous studies; as in Study 1 and Study 2, ToM questions increase with age (Pearson's $\chi^2(2) = 12.949$, $p < .002$). And while the percentages here are slightly smaller overall than for three of the four children in the CHILDES study (Study 1), they are very similar to the rates seen in the diary study (Study 2). So, the data from this study indicate that children this age are asking ToM questions with respect to animals, and thus this is evidence that children do consider animals to be appropriate candidates for questions about ToM. If a child asks a ToM question about an object, we can safely argue that they believe that object to have a mind, to be capable of thoughts, desires, and the like, or at least that they are considering the possibility that the object has these capabilities. So, it seems likely that children this age do seem to believe, or at least are considering it a possibility, that animals are capable of ToM processes, to whatever degree these children understand ToM processes at their current age.

The third prediction concerned activity questions. Did children ask more about activities than in the other studies? Table 19 shows that this did not happen, and in fact children asked slightly fewer questions about activities (although this slight decrease may simply be due to a larger number of label questions hogging up the percentages). Why didn't children ask more activity questions, despite being engaged with a set of stimulus items should have lent themselves particularly to such questions? Animals engage in a variety of activities, while inanimate objects do not; notice that even when animals are still, they are interpreted as sleeping, which would be considered an activity (and coded as such). Not so for a ball, for example, that might "roll" at one time, but not at another; when a ball is still, it is not perceived as being engaged in an activity. Simply because animals are always perceived as being engaged in some activity, why are there not more activity questions here?

There are two possible reasons for this. One is that children might actually show no real difference in the type of questions they ask about the activities of animate and inanimate objects; this would be surprising, and disconcerting, because children need to learn important things about what makes biological and nonbiological entities different from one another, and self-initiated activities are a part of this. The other possibility has to do with the coding system; the coding system was designed to capture an understanding of some basic aspects of objects that children might be asking about things in their environment—*all* things in their environment. While this

73

system might capture some differences between different types objects, it is not necessarily designed to capture these differences, differences like self-initiated activities (a dog walking) as opposed to other-initiated activities (a ball rolling, which is caused by an agent acting on the ball). So, this general coding system, because it was designed for a broader variety of items, may simply fail to capture this important distinction about biologically related phenomena. We cannot draw distinguish these possibilities with the current data analysis.

Do Children Ask Questions About Biological Phenomena?

One primary purpose of this study is to examine how children might be using questions to gather information about a specific domain, naïve biology. Previous work (reviewed above) suggests that as early as 4, children begin making important shifts in their understanding of biological knowledge. The model presented in this paper argues that children's questions may help them move toward more adult-like knowledge states; if this is so, children just before and at this age should be asking questions about biological phenomena. We'd expect that a situation involving animals would be an opportunity for them to explore this information if this is the case. Further, we'd expect the younger children to ask fewer questions about biological phenomena, and would expect older children who are closer to important shifts in this domain to be more inquisitive about this area. If this domain is not of particular interest to them at this time, we would not expect children's questions at any of the three ages to be particularly mindful of biological phenomena, but would expect them to focus instead on things like the names of the animals, appearances, properties, and part information at all ages.

What do we find when we look at specifically biologically related questions? Do children ask for more such questions when dealing with animals than they do in broader circumstances? Figure 34 shows the number of questions that asked for biological information in the real animal condition of the zoo data versus the CHILDES data, at each age. At all ages, children asked significantly more questions about biologically related phenomena when at the zoo (2;0–2;9: $\chi^2(1) = 5.33$, $p < .021$; 3;0–3;9: $\chi^2(1) = 12.5$, $p < .000$; 4;0–4;9: $\chi^2(1) = 12.5$, $p < .000$). So, children use the opportunity to ask about biological phenomena even though they do not necessarily have to do so, and could rather have asked more general questions about the animals; their exploration of biological phenomena increases in this more focused situation. Also, children's biologically related questions increased between the ages of 2 and 3, and hold strong at age 4 as they get closer to the age where they will be making important transitions in this area (Pearson's $\chi^2(2) = 10.41$, $p < .005$). This fits with the findings in the naïve biology

74

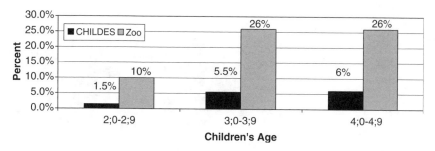

FIGURE 34.—Number of questions asking for biological information.

literature; we would expect them to be gathering information before this time that could help fuel relevant transitions in this area.

Further, a big part of what seems to shift in the naïve biology literature beginning around age 4 has to do with the core explanatory principles of this domain. If this is so, we would expect to see a lot of explanatory questions about biological phenomena; in fact, we would predict that this domain would be more of a target for explanatory questions than children's questions in general if this is an important domain to them at this time. Figure 35 shows the percentage of biological questions in the real animal condition of the zoo data set that ask for explanatory information, and the percentage of nonbiological questions that ask for explanatory information in this data set. At all ages, children ask for significantly more explanatory information when they are asking about biological phenomena than when they are not asking about biological phenomena (2;0–2;9: $\chi^2(1) = 6.25$, $p < .012$; 3;0–3;9: $\chi^2(1) = 4.25, p < .039$; 4;0–4;9: $\chi^2(1) = 7.23, p < .007$). This difference remains strong at each age (Pearson's $\chi^2(2) = 1.66$, $p = .437$). Further, the percentage of explanatory biological questions asked by the child rises steadily with age (Pearson's $\chi^2(2) = 20.86$, $p < .000$), and in fact reaches almost half of the questions asked about biological information—a much higher rate of explanatory questions than seen anywhere else in this paper.

Note that it is not the case that some general increase in explanatory questions overall is responsible for the high rate of explanatory questions here; if it were, we would see similar levels of explanatory questions asked among the biological questions and the nonbiological questions. This also is not due to a new-found ability to ask causal questions; children are asking causal questions at the youngest age, and the ability to form causal questions logically does not change across domains ("Why?" is effective in any domain). What's changing here are the relative percentages of causal questions regarding the domain of biology. So, as children get older, they are asking more about biological phenomena, and at each age children are asking a higher percentage than overall of questions that correspond to the

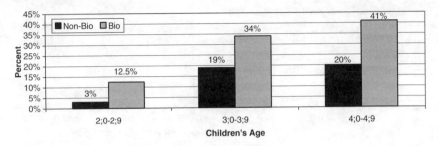

FIGURE 35.—Percentage of biological versus nonbiological questions that ask for explanatory information (real animal condition).

"deeper" part of concept formation regarding biological information, information that directly relates to a shift in conceptual understanding that they are on the cusp of making.

How Does Stimulus Type Affect Children's Questions About Biological Knowledge?

The parent/child dyads went through one of three different zoos; one with real animals, one with drawings of those same animals, and one with three dimensional, realistic replicas of those animals. In much of the literature on biological knowledge (and in other literatures), there is an implicit assumption that drawings, pictures, or replicas of animals are an adequate stand-in for real animals. Did the difference in stimulus type have an effect on the biological questions children asked? Figure 36 shows the percentage of biological questions asked by children in each of the three conditions. Children who observed real animals were significantly more likely to ask questions regarding biological phenomena than were children who observed drawings or replicas of animals, except in one case (real vs. drawings: 2;0–2;9: $\chi^2(1) = 3.77$, $p < .052$; 3;0–3;9: $\chi^2(1) = 4.33$, $p < .037$; 4;0–4;9:

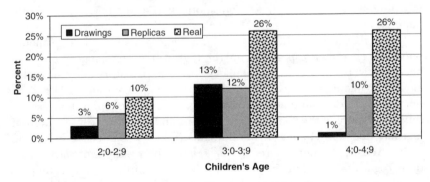

FIGURE 36.—Percentage of biological questions asked regarding live animals, pictures, and, replicas.

$\chi^2(1) = 23.15, p < .000$; real vs. replicas: 2;0–2;9: $\chi^2(1) = 1.00, p = .317$; 3;0–3;9: $\chi^2(1) = 5.16, p < .023$; 4;0–4;9: $\chi^2(1) = 7.11, p < .008$). Recall that this is not due to activities that the real animals are engaged in, because the drawings of animals show just as many (if not more) animals engaged in the same range of activities. It also is not due to the realistic colors, shapes, textures, and parts of the real animals, because the replicas of the animals have these properties. However, something about the real animals leads children to ask more questions about biological phenomena; this seems to indicate a different type of engagement on the part of children when dealing with real animals. This has implications for what children might be learning from these stimuli, and what we can learn about children's knowledge when using these stimuli.

So, the amount of biological information that children request is greatly reduced when they are interacting with pictures or replicas rather than real animals. What about those questions they do still ask in these conditions, are they altered by stimulus type in any way? Above (in Figure 34) we see that when asking biological questions about real animals, children ask a higher percentage of explanatory information than when asking nonbiological questions. Does stimulus type change this? Figures 37 and 38 shows the answer to this is yes. In two cases, children continue to ask significantly more explanatory questions when asking about biological phenomenon, out of the much reduced number of biological questions that they do ask in these conditions (drawings, 3;0–3;9: $\chi^2(1) = 33.82, p < .000$; replicas 3;0–3;9: $\chi^2(1) = 17.78, p < .000$). However, in the remaining cases, children ask the same number of explanatory questions (drawings 2;0–2;9: $\chi^2(1) = 0.00, p = 1$; replicas 2;0–2;9: $\chi^2(1) = 0.33, p = .564$), or fewer explanatory questions (drawings 4;0–4;9: $\chi^2(1) = 7.36, p < .007$; replicas 4;0–4;9: $\chi^2(1) = 12.25, p < .000$). This again represents a large impact of the stimulus type on the cognitive engagement of the children.

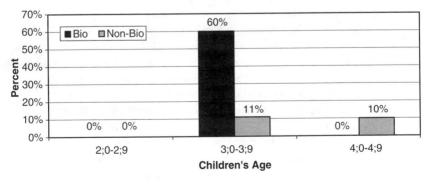

FIGURE 37.—Percentage of explanatory biological questions in the drawings condition.

77

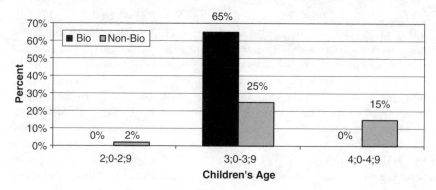

FIGURE 38.—Percentage of explanatory biological questions in the replicas condition.

Let's look more closely at the progression of this change. Remember that the percentage of questions asking about biological phenomena increases at ages 3 and 4, but that at all ages, children ask more explanatory questions when asking about biological phenomena than they do when asking about nonbiological phenomena. For 2-year-olds, who ask the fewest biological questions to start with, drawings/replicas first decrease the number of biological questions they ask, and further reduce the explanatory quality of the biological questions. So, these children are asking few biological questions, and fewer questions that could be deepening their causal understanding of the domain. Recall that at approximately age 3 there is a spike in explanatory questions across domains (see Figures 8–11, 19, 30). So, while 3-year-olds are asking fewer biological questions when dealing with drawings/replicas, this strong focus on explanatory information that we see across all of their questions, along with their increased focus on biological phenomena, seems to keep the number of explanatory questions here high; the result is that while they are asking many fewer biological questions, the ones they do ask still contain questions that are conceptually "deep," despite the impoverished stimulus items.

The most dramatic shift occurs at age 4; these children show the greatest interest in explanatory information regarding the domain of biology (Figure 35), and this seems to fit with what we know of the progress of the domain of naïve biology—this is the time when children's understanding of this domain is about to begin to shift, so it is not surprising to see so many questions regarding the underlying causal principles of the domain. However, drawings and pictures seem to be particularly deleterious to these children's exploration of the domain of biology. Not only are they asking fewer question about biology overall, but those that they do ask are now *less* likely to be asking for explanatory information when thinking about biological phenomena, despite the fact that they are *at their most likely* to ask for explanatory information when looking at real animals, across all ages; because of this greater interest in explanatory biological information when looking at real animals, we know the drop we see with drawings/replicas is not simply due to the children having learned what they need to know, and no longer being interested causally in this domain—they are still very much interested when looking at real animals. So, at an important time in the development of biological knowledge, when the children seem to be especially interested in biological phenomena, the type of stimulus materials the children are looking at seems to result in a qualitative difference in the type of cognitive engagement the children have with the stimuli. This again may have consequences for how children learn with materials such as these, and may have consequences for the data gathered by research that uses stimulus materials other than real animals.

DISCUSSION

The first primary goal of Study 3 was to examine how children's questions relate to the conceptual developments they are making in one specific domain. Thus, the data in this study allowed in-depth analysis of one given content area, questions about animals. Around the age of 4, children begin to show shifts in their conceptual understandings of biological phenomena; if questions are playing a role in helping them to gather information about this domain, we would expect to see that reflected in the questions they ask just before and around the time of this shift. A setting focused on animals should provide them an opportunity to ask questions about biological phenomena; if they are not yet puzzling out these issues, their questions would not tap into these issues, and might instead focus only on nonbiological issues, like the names of the animals, their appearances, where they are located, and so on. The results show that when engaged with animals, children do ask for much more biological information than in other settings, so when the opportunity presents itself, children's curiosity about this domain comes out. These questions increase as they get older, as we would predict as they move towards the age where we know the conceptual shifts in this domain begin to occur. Further, we find that when asking about biological information, they are more likely to ask for explanatory information about the domain than when asking about nonbiological information. In this way, their questions show a differential sensitivity to where they focus on causal information; they differentiate between more general information about animals, and information that may be helping them solve biologically related issues—these issues engage them in a different way conceptually. The questions they are asking gather information that is relevant and potentially useful to the conceptual shift they will soon be making, or have just started to make.

The second primary goal of this study was to examine the impact of different types of stimulus items on children's engagement and potential learning via questions. This study, unlike Studies 1 and 2, allowed the separation of different types of objects: real objects versus representation of objects (drawings and three-dimensional replicas). The results showed that children engage very differently with these different stimulus types; children asked fewer questions about biological information when looking at representations of animals, and asked fewer causal questions when looking at representations of animals, particularly at the oldest age. These data suggest that representations are different in important ways from real objects, and that because of this, children may learn differently when interacting with them. They ask fewer questions and different questions when engaged with representations, and thus gather different information about animals. Because of this difference in engagement, we have to be cautious when using representations to gauge children's knowledge about domains that may be highly affected by stimulus type, as is the domain of biology, where important information may not be preserved over different stimulus types.

The secondary goal of Study 3 was to use a third methodology to test predictions about the basic requirements of the information requesting mechanism. Study 3 also found that the vast majority of children's questions are seeking information, and these information-seeking questions occur with remarkable frequency—in this study, the children ask an average of 95 questions an hour, or three questions every 2 minutes. While it is not clear if this is due to a more one-on-one focus in this study between parent and child or a greater engagement with the particular stimulus items of this study, what is clear is that the frequency of questions reported in study one are not due to the small number of subjects in that study. It also is not an artifact of the type of methodology used, or the situations those children were in.

Parents were again very responsive to their children, answering their questions as much as 86% of the time, and adding additional information as much as 13% of the time; these rates correspond almost exactly those found in Studies 1 and 2. Further, children in this study were just as likely to persist as were the children in study 1; they keep asking for information when they get a response that is not informative, and stop asking when they get a response that is informative. So here again, the children are not just trying to get the parents' attention, they also are genuinely concerned with getting the information they asked about.

At all ages, children's questions again primarily ask for facts, but in the older age groups, more and more of the children's questions ask for explanatory information, as seen in Studies 1 and 2. This also holds within a particular exchange; children ask both isolated questions and questions that occur in a series that build on one another, and it is the building questions that are more likely to shift from fact questions to more explanatory information. These findings again parallel the shift in questions seen in adults learning about a topic. In addition to validating these findings, this study, via the targeted exploration of biological questions, further suggests that learning may be occurring in these ways. The increase in explanatory questions relevant to the target domain just before the time we know children to make relevant advances in the domain offers temporally contiguous support for the argument that these questions could be contributing to the shifts that will come in children's thinking; the fact that the questions start before the shift and not after it points toward the direction of causality. However, it is crucial to note that while temporal contiguity is suggestive, it certainly is not conclusive, and should not be overinterpreted.

Overall, despite a third different methodology, the general content of the questions children ask in the study remained similar to that reported in Studies 2 and 3; this is further validation that these studies are tapping into something real about the general content that interests children. In addition to this, three predictions were made about shifts that would occur with respect to the general content of children questions. As predicted, the decline in children's questions about labels that was found in Studies 1 and 2 disappeared in this study, due to a number of novel animals among the stimulus items. This suggests that in addition to general shifts in the use of the IRM due to the cognitive advances the child is making, the child also adapts to the need of any given situation, asking for whatever information is needed at the current time effectively.

A second prediction concerned ToM questions; children's ToM questions in this study were used as a diagnostic of which entities children considered capable of mental processes. The presence of similar amounts of ToM questions in this study suggests that children believe animals to be proper targets for questions on this topic—they believe that animals have ToM processes, or at least they are exploring this possibility. This provides a tantalizing example of how the data from these studies, along with more focused studies, could be used to gather quantifiable data regarding the current state of children's conceptual structures—what they do or do not believe about a given topic/domain/knowledge area. This is one direction that future studies in this area should absolutely take.

The findings of these first three studies, although gathered under very different circumstances and using very different methodologies, strongly validate one another. This greatly decreases any likelihood that the results are a function of the particular children involved in any one of the studies (a particularly important concern in the CHILDES study, which consists of data from only four children), are limited to a particular situation (as the diary data span a large variety of situations), or are artifacts due to the methodological limitations of any one of the studies. The patterns reported here document real phenomena, and support the existence of the IRM and its potential value to children for resolving the problems they encounter on the path to an adult-like understanding of the world.

However, while these studies show that children are certainly capable of gathering information they need efficiently by asking questions, and that the information they ask for seems to be related to their cognitive advances, we cannot draw conclusions about causality from these data. While it seems unlikely that all of this information is only being coincidentally requested and produced, and does not have an effect on the children's developing conceptual structures, there is no evidence here of any actual impact on any conceptual structure—there is no evidence that any of the information children get from asking questions actually goes in, and/or is used for some purpose, and accomplishes some goal. Study 4 is a laboratory experiment designed to target this issue.

V. DO CHILDREN'S QUESTIONS CHANGE THEIR KNOWLEDGE STATE?

While Studies 1–3 found that children ask hundreds of questions each day that gather information, and that they get answers to the vast majority of these questions, there is no evidence that children are asking these questions purposefully to address some problem or issue, or that the children successfully use the information they get in some productive way. If the questions that preschoolers so copiously ask are having a benefit for their cognitive development, they must be using them purposefully to gather information that they then use in some way, in a way that has an effect on their conceptual structures and/or immediate problem solving. The model presented in this paper asserts that when children encounter a "problem" (some gap in knowledge, some ambiguity, etc.) between the world and their current knowledge state, this leads to disequilibrium, and they can ask a question to get the information they need, use this information as needed, and resolve the disequilibrium. But how do we know that children can employ questions purposefully, and that children are using the information they get as a result of a question in a strategic manner? The model presented in this monograph suggests that children's questions are designed to target disequilibrium caused by problems such as a gap in knowledge or an ambiguous situation—can preschoolers ask questions in a way that allows them to address a problem? Are they tapping into their existing conceptual knowledge to assess the situation and ask a question that will solve the current problem for them? And can they use information they have gathered productively in some way? Study 4 examines these issues by testing whether or not children can recruit needed information to successfully solve a task at hand.

STUDY 4: METHODS

Participants

A total of 67 children, 35 children aged 4;0–4;10 (mean age 4;4) and 32 children aged 5;0–5;9 (mean age 5;3), participated. Children this age were chosen because they are in the preschool range of children used in our previous studies, and are old enough to navigate the complexities of this task; this will be discussed further below. Participants were drawn from the population of Bing Nursery school.

Procedure

Overview: Children were shown a box, along with two pictures of different objects. They were told that the box contained one of the two objects shown in the pictures. In the experimental condition (the "question" condition), children were told the point of the game was to guess what was hidden in the box; these children were allowed to ask any questions they wanted in order to figure out which item was in the box. In the control condition (the "guess" condition), they were told the point of the game was to guess what was hidden in the box; these children were not allowed to ask questions. Both conditions began with one demonstration trial, where the child got to hide one of two objects, and the experimenter asked questions/ guessed what was in the box (depending on condition). If the child did not understand the demonstration trial (e.g., if they hid both objects in the box) or had impulse-control failures (if they showed the hidden object before the experimenter guessed) or if they played according to their own rules (e.g., playing a trick on the experimenter by answering the questions incorrectly), the demonstration trial was repeated again. If the child still did not understand the demonstration trial and/or did not play by the rules, the child was excluded from the study. For the most part, these problems were not an issue with 4- and 5-year-old children; six children were excluded for not following the rules during the demonstration trial, but for five out of these six, this was because they tried to trick the experimenter during the demonstration trial, and not because they did not understand the rules or had problems with impulse control. However, younger children (3-year-olds) often did not understand the rules and did things like hide both objects in the box, or had impulse-control issues and would show us what they had hidden in the box right away, disqualifying them for participation in the study. While these younger children had no problems generating questions, these procedural issues made this task inappropriate for them.

After the demonstration trial, during the "question" condition, six target trials followed. The child was told it was now their turn to play. The experimenter showed two new pictures, and had the child identify them. The experimenter then had the child cover their eyes, and hid one of the two pictured objects in the box (making sure the child was not peeking). The experimenter then asked the child if they would like to ask a question to figure out what was in the box, or just guess. For each question, the child was given a truthful answer, and then the child was asked if they would like to ask another question, or if they were ready to guess what was in the box.

Once the child indicated they were ready to guess and did so, the experimenter showed them what was in the box.

For the "guess" condition, the trials proceeded as in the "question" condition, except that rather than being asked if they would like to ask a question, children were asked to guess which object they thought was hidden in the box. If they tried to ask a question, they were told that they were supposed to guess. After the child guessed, the experimenter showed them what was in the box, and the trials continued, again for a total of six trials.[7]

For each of the trials, the stimulus pairs that were presented to the child got more difficult, in that they were more similar to each other, and so were harder to differentiate. The first two stimulus pairs presented were of low similarity (e.g., "cat" vs. "ball," where a cat is a natural kind, a ball is an artifact, a cat can move on its own, both are highly perceptually dissimilar, etc.), the second two were moderately similar (e.g., "cat" vs. "duck," where both are now natural kinds, but cats walk while ducks swim, cats have four feet, while ducks have two, etc.), and the final two were of high similarity (e.g., "cat" and "dog" both are animals, walk on four feet, are common pets, etc.), making it progressively harder to find a question that would differentiate the two objects (these similarity rankings were verified by adult subjects). The following stimulus sets were used (Table 20).

Presentation of the stimuli was counterbalanced for the order of presentation, such that no sets habitually followed one another; the order of similarity between the target item and mate (so that each target item was presented with mates of large, medium, and small similarity over the course of the study); and whether the target object or the nontarget object was placed in the box.

DATA ANALYSIS AND RESULTS

Does the Opportunity to Ask Questions Allow Children to Solve the Problem?

The number of items correctly identified by each child were averaged over the six stimulus trials, and ANOVA analyses were used to test for significant differences between conditions, ages, and gender.

Were children who were allowed to ask questions able to assess the situation, generate a question that would appropriately differentiate the stimulus materials, and then employ the information successfully to identify the object? Children could fail at this in a number of ways. First, they might ask a question that is pragmatically inappropriate; for example, if they ask "is it something I have at home?" or "is it beautiful?", the experimenter would have no way of knowing what the child has at home, or what the child believes is beautiful. Experimenters were instructed to answer truthfully in these cases; so, if the child were to ask "is it beautiful," and the experimenter

TABLE 20
STIMULUS MATERIALS

Target item	Low similarity	Moderate similarity	High similarity
Drum (demonstration)	Drum vs. watch		
Cat	Cat vs. ball	Cat vs. bird	Cat vs. dog
Truck	Truck vs. snake	Truck vs. boat	Truck vs. car
Apple	Apple vs. bucket	Apple vs. pizza	Apple vs. orange
Spoon	Spoon vs. bicycle	Spoon vs. cup	Spoon vs. fork
Chair	Chair vs. carrot	Chair vs. table	Chair vs. couch
Rose	Rose vs. dolly	Rose vs. plant	Rose vs. daisy

thought it was, she would say yes. If the child were to ask "Is it something I have at home?" the experimenter would answer "I do not know." Second, the child might ask a question that is pragmatically appropriate, but fails to appropriately differentiate the two objects at hand; for example, if the child is trying to differentiate the spoon and the fork, and they ask "is it for eating?," this will not differentiate the objects for the child, because both items are for eating. Third, the child might not ask any questions at all, either because they are incapable (which seems unlikely given the overwhelming number of questions reported in the observational studies) or because they just want to cut to the chase and guess what is in the box. Finally, children might ask an appropriate question and get an answer that differentiates the objects, but might fail to use that information correctly; for example, if they ask "is it for eating cereal," and the experimenter says "no," they should then conclude that the object in the box is the fork. If they then guess that they object is the spoon, they have failed to correctly use the information they have recruited.

Children can, and do, make all of these errors; 1 child asked a pragmatically inappropriate question ("is it beautiful?"); 13 children asked questions that failed to differentiate the objects on one or more of their trials; seven children chose to guess rather than ask questions on all of their trials, and two more guessed on some of their trials without asking questions; two children failed to use the information they had gathered correctly, choosing the object that was not indicated by the answers they had received. So, the opportunity to ask questions here does not logically entail that children will do better than if they are not given the opportunity to ask questions; there are many ways this opportunity can fail them.

It is important to point out that children were not told that they *had* to ask a question, and they were not forced to do so; if they wanted to just guess, they could. In fact, the utterance posed to children gave them a choice between asking a question and guessing. As noted above, several children did not ask questions, suggesting that there was not an over-arching task demand that forced children to do something they would not normally do; this task did not artificially ensure that children would ask questions. Another indication of this is that all but four of the children who asked questions asked more than one question on at least one trial, indicating that they were not just asking a question to satisfy the experimenter, but asked questions until they believed they had enough information to determine what was in the box.

So, despite the many ways that children could fail at this task, did children use questions to successfully identify the hidden object? Figure 39 shows that children in the question condition were significantly better at identifying which item was in the box than children in the guess condition (for the 4-year-olds, $F = 10.415$, $p < .003$; for the 5-year-olds, $F = 18.16$, $p < .000$). This does not differ between the two ages ($F = .453$, $p = .503$), and there is no difference between the performance of males and females (main effect: $F = .035$, $p = .885$; gender by condition interaction: $F = .099$, $p = .755$). So, from the youngest age presented here, children are able to generate appropriate questions which recruit the necessary information to solve this problem, and then employ that information effectively.

For all of the remaining analyses, children's questions were coded as indicated below, tabulated, and chi-square analyses were performed to test differences between the frequencies.

How Effective Are Children's Questions?

Children asked 267 questions in the course of this study; 4-year-olds asked 138 questions, while the 5-year-olds asked 129 questions. How many of these questions were appropriate to the task at hand, and actually solved the problem for them? Figure 40 shows that the overwhelming majority of the questions that children generate are appropriate for differentiating the

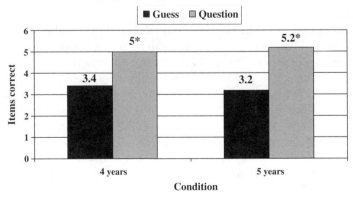

FIGURE 39.—Number of items identified correctly by children.

87

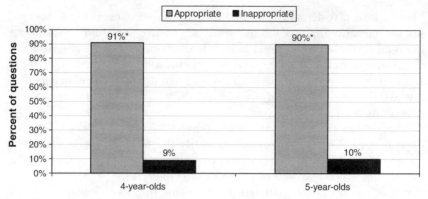

FIGURE 40.—Percent of questions that appropriately differentiate the stimulus items.

objects in question (for the 4-year-olds, $\chi^2(1) = 91.86$, $p < .000$; for the 5-year-olds, $\chi^2(1) = 80.32$, $p < .000$). This does not change over the age groups (Pearson's $\chi^2(1) = .059$, $p = .808$). Both groups of preschoolers are able to assess the situation at hand and generate a question that adequately gathers information and solves the problem for them.

What happens when children ask an inappropriate question, one that does not gather the needed information for them? Are they able to recognize this, and ask another question? In the data set, 23 of the questions the children asked were inappropriate questions, ones that would not solve the problem for the child. Out of these, children recovered by asking an appropriate follow-up question 12 out of 23 of these times. So, roughly half of the time, children are able to recognize that the first question did not get the information they needed, and ask again. What is happening in the remaining 11 cases? Because children overwhelmingly succeed at asking appropriate questions, their skill at asking questions does not seem to be the issue, so possibly some other cognitive ability may be playing a role here. One likely candidate is the difficulty involved in considering/holding two options in mind simultaneously; younger children in particular struggle with this, and will tend to perseverate on one of the options at hand to the neglect of the other (Kirkham, Cruess, & Diamond, 2003; Zelazo, Frye, & Rapus, 1996). Are the younger children perseverating on one of the two target items only, failing to realize that the answer they have received could apply to both items? For example, when faced with the fork and the spoon, they may be looking only at the fork when they ask "is it for eating," and because of this, when they get a yes response they will take this as confirmation that the fork must be hidden in the box, because they are failing to consider the spoon. This possibility is supported when we break down the data by age; 4-year-olds recover from the error only four out of 11 times

88

(36%), while 5-year-olds recover nine out of 12 times (75%). because children are highly skilled at asking questions equally at both age, relative skill in generating questions cannot account for this difference, but if younger children are more likely to perseverate on one item only, this is the pattern of results we would expect to find. Unfortunately, there are not enough data points to analyze statistically here, so these data are descriptive only and must be considered, and interpreted, with caution.

Are children more successful when they ask more questions? The vast majority of failure trials were due to children who decided to cut to the chase and guess what was in the box, rather than ask any questions. But what about the children who did ask questions, did asking multiple questions increase their likelihood of success? On the trials where children failed to identify the hidden object, they asked 1.4 questions. On the trials where children were successful, they asked 1.6 questions. The number of questions asked by children on success trials does not differ by age; both 4- and 5-year-olds ask 1.6 questions on average before succeeding. So, it does not seem like number of questions is the key; asking the right question seems to be the key. However, these data should be interpreted with caution, as there is not enough power to analyze them statistically, due to the very small number of trials on which children asked a question, but still failed to identify the object correctly.

What Information Do Children Use to Solve the Problem?

What types of questions are children asking to differentiate the objects? What aspect of the stimulus items are they using to solve the problem? The questions children asked fell into three coding categories: questions asking about the function of an object, which included both functions for artifacts and habitual activities for animals ("Does it drive on the road?," "Does it meow?"); questions about parts of objects ("Does it have ears?"); and questions about properties of objects ("Is it yellow?," "Does it smell good?"). All of the questions clearly fell into these three categories, and reliability for these codes and for the others presented in this chapter, were at 95% agreement or higher. Figure 41 shows the percentages of each type of question asked by the children. Function questions were the majority of children's questions, with part questions coming in second, and property questions comprising the lowest percentage of children's questions.

The model proposed in this paper argues that when children are learning about the world and using questions to gather and apply knowledge, they are comparing what they currently know about a concept/category/domain with the situation at hand, and requesting information they need to fill in any blanks and/or resolve any inconsistencies they encounter. One of the strengths of the procedure used here is that it allows children to

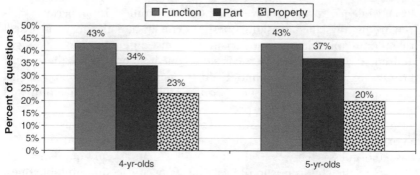

FIGURE 41.—Percentage of function, part, and property questions asked by children.

tap into their conceptual knowledge about the target items they were considering. For example, they might tap into the conceptual knowledge they have about cats and balls, pull up facts about these items (that cats meow and balls don't, and that balls are for rolling, and cats aren't), and ask questions based on the facts they were able to retrieve ("does it meow?" and/ or "can you roll it?"). On the other hand, even though they have the opportunity to do this, they might simply use perceptual information ("is it white?" or "is it pink?") that requires no conceptual information at all; if the objects in the pictures were nonsense objects that the children had never seen before, the children would still be able to use color to ask about which object was in the box, despite having no conceptual structure with respect to these objects. In fact, using perceptual information would always be the easier choice for children, because it does not require activating a conceptual structure and picking out a relevant piece of information that applies to one object but not the other; for this reason, we would expect children to more often take the easy way out, and simply use perceptual features to differentiate the two objects, rather than trying to employ existing conceptual information to solve the problem.

Did children ask questions that tapped into their relevant knowledge structures, or did they simply latch onto obvious perceptual features? Figure 42 shows the percentage of the children's questions that asked about conceptual information (aspects of the object that were not simply visible from the picture), and the percentage of children's questions that asked for information that could be seen in the pictures. This graph shows that despite having an easier strategy for solving the problem, children ask just as many questions that require tapping into conceptual knowledge about the objects at hand, with no significant difference between questions asking about visible and nonvisible information (for 4-year-olds, $\chi^2(1) = .583$, $p = .445$; for 5-year-olds, $\chi^2(1) = .071$, $p = .790$). This does not change with age (Pearson's $\chi^2(1) = .112$, $p = .737$). Because children have an easier out,

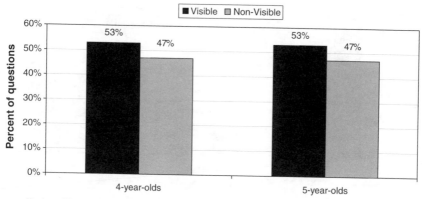

FIGURE 42.—Percent of questions asking about visible versus nonvisible properties of objects.

but are just as likely to go a more complicated way, accessing the existing conceptual knowledge in order to try to solve the situation at hand is a natural strategy they bring to asking questions in order to solve problems in the world.

Further, taking the more difficult strategy of asking about conceptual information rather than the easier-to-access perceptual information may actually reduce children's likelihood of succeeding. When children ask a question but still fail to succeed on the trial, in 77% of these cases, children asked for conceptual information rather then perceptual information. On trials where they succeed after asking a question, 45% of those questions asked for conceptual information. However, this data must be considered with extreme caution due to the very small number of questions that lead to failure.

What happens when we push children's ability by making the stimulus items more difficult to differentiate? As noted above, the stimulus sets children received differ in their level of similarity, with each child receiving two items that were of low similarity, two items that were of moderate similarity, and two items that were of high similarity. When the objects are more similar, and therefore more difficult to differentiate, it may become harder for the children to find criteria during their search of existing conceptual structures that will differentiate the two items adequately; if this happens, children may switch strategies, and find another source of information that can help them solve the problem at hand. Figure 43 shows the percent of each question type children ask for each level of similarity:

The type of questions 4-year-olds ask does indeed change as the stimulus sets get harder to differentiate (Pearson's $\chi^2(4) = 24.83$, $p < .000$). When stimulus sets are of low similarity, and thus are easy to differentiate, children are more likely to ask questions about functions, and are less likely

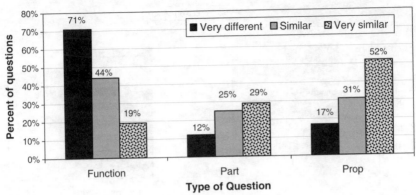

FIGURE 43.—Percent of each question type 4-year-olds requested at different levels of stimulus similarity.

to ask for parts and properties of the objects. However, as the stimulus sets become more similar, and thus harder to differentiate, questions about object function become less likely than questions asking for properties or parts of objects. Figure 44 shows that the same is true of 5-year-olds, although the trend is less pronounced. While the overall statistic is only approaching significance (Pearson's $\chi^2(4) = 7.851, p = .091$), when the stimulus sets are of low similarity, a question is significantly more likely to be asking for function information ($\chi^2(2) = 12.47, p < .002$), when they are of moderate similarity, there is no difference between the type of information children request ($\chi^2(2) = 2.29, p = .319$), and when they are of high similarity, a question is significantly most likely to be asking for property information ($\chi^2(2) = 6.14$,

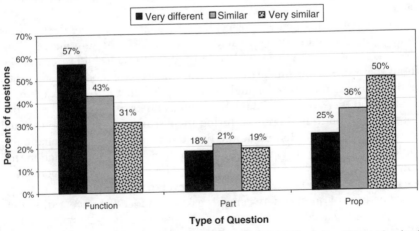

FIGURE 44.—Percent of each question type 5-year-olds requested at different levels of stimulus similarity.

$p < .046$). So, as stimulus sets get more difficult to differentiate, children are changing their strategies, in the same way at both ages. This suggests that children start out trying to solve the problem by searching their existing conceptual knowledge, and if/when this fails, they look for a different strategy. Children's skill in asking questions, then, is strong and flexible; they assess the situation, tap into their conceptual information when they can, and adjust their strategy as need be to solve the problem facing them.

So children do ask for different sorts of information as the stimulus sets get more difficult to differentiate, but is this really a matter of a conceptual strategy versus a perceptual one? Not all property questions are necessarily asking for purely visible information, for example asking "does it smell good" of a rose is a property question, but this property is not visible. Similarly, asking "does it have a steering wheel" of a car if the steering wheel is not pictured in the photo, is not asking about perceptual information, but rather is drawing on the child's conceptual knowledge of what parts a car has. If we would like to know whether children are relying on conceptual information or perceptual information, we need to look at cases where children are asking about aspects of the objects that are visible in the photos versus aspects that are not visible. Figure 45 shows what we find when we code the children's questions in this way.

For 4-year-olds, when stimulus sets are very different, and therefore easy to differentiate, a question is more likely to be asking about nonvisible properties ($\chi^2(1) = 8.40$, $p < .004$), when the items are somewhat similar,

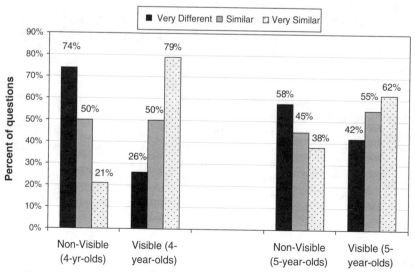

FIGURE 45.—Percent of children's questions asking for visible versus nonvisible information.

children are just as likely to use either type of information ($\chi^2(1) = 0, p = 1$), and when the items are very similar and difficult to differentiate, children are more likely to rely on visible properties to identify the object ($\chi^2(1) = 16.33, p < .000$). For 5-year-olds, although there is a slight trend to asking more for visual information when the items are most similar, this trend does not reach significance, and at all similarity levels the children are just as likely to ask questions about nonvisible properties as they are to ask about visible properties (low similarity, $\chi^2(1) = 1.14, p = .286$; moderate similarity, $\chi^2(1) = .381, p = .537$; high similarity, $\chi^2(1) = 2.38, p = .123$). The findings for the 4-year-olds and the trend in the data for the 5-year-olds again suggest that children's question-asking strategies change with the situation at hand; they are able to change their strategy in order to obtain information that will solve the problem for them, even when they do not have the relevant conceptual knowledge at hand. The weaker trend in the case of the 5-year-olds is not surprising, because they have greater conceptual knowledge, and are likely not being taxed as strongly as 4-year-olds, who don't know quite as much about things as 5-year-olds do.

So in light of this, the data seen in Figure 42 do not seem to indicate an equal likelihood to use either conceptual or perceptual strategies; what seems to be happening is that children begin searching their conceptual knowledge, and when their current conceptual knowledge is not sufficient to allow them to differentiate the stimulus sets (more likely in the case of 4-year-olds who have less conceptual knowledge), they switch strategies, and find another source of information to use that can help them solve the problem at hand. This shows that tapping into an existing conceptual store to generate a question is a natural part of question-asking; it also shows a strength and flexibility in children's skill at asking questions that adapts to the situation at hand and allows children to gather the information they need effectively.

However, there is also an alternative explanation here. The level of stimulus similarity was not counterbalanced for order of presentation; children always got the easiest items first, and the hardest items last, to prevent them from being overwhelmed with very difficult stimulus sets while they were still becoming accustomed to the task. So, it is possible that children were getting fatigued here, rather than more challenged with respect to the stimulus sets. This possibility seems less likely—if children were tired, they could skip the questions entirely and simply guess—but it cannot be ruled out and must be seriously considered. However, this is, in essence, the same argument—as the task gets more difficult for the children, whether because they are having more difficulty generating dimensions on which the stimulus items differ, or they are getting more tired, they switch strategies and ask more questions about perceptual information. What is key here is that while using perceptual information is always the easier strategy, this is not where children start; they start by searching their conceptual structures, and move away from this strategy when the going gets rougher. This suggests that checking out what one already knows and matching it up to current circumstances is the default when trying to figure out a given situation.

Discussion

Studies 1–3 found that children ask a large number of questions in the course of their day, that they receive informative responses to the majority of these questions, and that the information they request could be useful for cognitive development. However, the nature of the studies reported there do not allow any causal link to be made; there is no evidence that children are asking these questions purposefully to solve some problem currently facing them, or that the information they receive is used in any way. If asking questions is a mechanism that children use during cognitive development to gather needed information to learn about the world and solve problems they encounter, evidence is needed that children can employ questions strategically in this way. Study 4 is designed to establish experimentally that children do have the ability to assess a situation, draw on their conceptual structures to formulate a question that will gather the needed information, and then apply the information they have gathered to solve the problem at hand. The results presented here indicate that children do have this ability—despite ample ways that the child could fail if not skilled in how to ask a good question and use the information correctly, children are more likely to identify the hidden objects correctly when they are allowed to ask questions about the objects.

Children are able to strategically generate good questions that appropriately differentiate the target objects, equally at both ages. They are able to draw upon their existing conceptual knowledge to generate dimensions on which the items differ, and use these dimensions to formulate an appropriate question. They do this despite the fact that using purely visible information would be easier than searching through their conceptual knowledge to solve the problem; this suggests that drawing on conceptual knowledge and comparing it to the current situation is a natural process for children when generating questions. When the task gets harder, either because the stimulus items become more difficult to differentiate and push the limits of the children's conceptual knowledge or the children are becoming fatigued, they are able to flexibly adapt by switching strategies, and find another dimension to ask about—information that is visibly available in the picture. Children are thus skilled at using whatever information they have at hand to efficiently generate a question and resolve a problem, and can compensate when their preexisting conceptual knowledge or energy level is not adequate for the task at hand.

The current study uses a task with an overt problem that needs to be solved—children need to get a piece of information in order to identify a hidden object. This task mirrors many of the tasks that face children throughout their day, in the course of play and daily activities. The task is also analogous to the covert "problems" that children are solving—for example, when they realize that they do not know what an object is called, they have identified a piece of information they are missing, and can ask a question to get that information. According to the model presented in this paper, a child who sees something they do not recognize asks "what is it?" and gets the response "a hammer" now has a change in knowledge state, via a single question—they now know that the object is called a hammer. In the case of this study, children identify a piece of information they are missing (what the object is in the box) and ask a question to get the information they need; this results in a change of knowledge state (they now know what is in the box) and they can use this information now as needed. Their ability to identify the object in the box gives us overt behavioral evidence of the change in knowledge state.

The fact that they can effectively apply the information they get in the overt task reported here suggests that they can likewise apply the information they get in such "covert" internal cases as getting the name for an unknown object, and use it to build appropriate knowledge structures.

A side note here involves the issue of stimulus type. Pictures were used in Study 4 to show children which of two objects might be in the box (the actual item in the box was a real object). So, when children were generating questions, they were engaged with pictures. In Study 3, the data suggested that stimulus type has an effect on the questions children ask, and more impoverished stimuli (pictures and 3-D replicas) had an effect on the questions children asked. On the surface, this seems to raise a contradiction; why were children in Study 4 capable of asking questions based on an "impoverished" stimulus set? First, the argument regarding stimulus type is a qualitative one, rather than a quantitative one. The argument is not necessarily that children will ask fewer questions when engaged with pictures or replicas; it is that they will ask *different* questions. Something about real objects allows a different type of engagement, theoretically because they have a richer source of cues that allow the person to tap into conceptual knowledge more efficiently, or more thoroughly (and in the domain of biology, this may have particularly important implications, because the type of information missing from pictures and replicas may be highly relevant to biological phenomena). If this is so, and pictures qualitatively change the questions children ask, how would this impact the outcome of Study 4? We would predict that pictures would make the task a bit harder, because there are fewer cues that help tap into the child's conceptual knowledge, and thus, search of those conceptual structures would be harder. This would work against the hypothesis, making it harder for children to generate questions, thus making it harder to succeed. We might also predict that children would ask qualitatively different questions if the study had used real objects; the only way to know this would be to run a condition using real objects outside of the box as well as inside of the box, and see what changes. However, any difference would only matter if the sort of questions children ask when looking at pictures did not help them solve to the problem, and that did not happen here. So, though children with these stimulus items may have, in theory, made the task more difficult, that would only make the findings here more conservative when evaluating children's question-asking abilities.

Studies 1 and 3 find that children ask more than a question a minute when engaged in conversation with adults; the data reported here suggest that these copious questions are employed strategically, and that children have the ability to use the information they receive to effectively resolve the conceptual problems they encounter when they explore the world. This would allow them to resolve internal disequilibrium and efficiently build knowledge structures, as well as solve immediate overt problems in their environment. And so, asking questions is a powerful mechanism that children can use to gather information that allows them to move forward on their journey toward an adult-like understanding of the world.

NOTE

7. At first glance, this control condition might seem unnecessary, as it may seem to be providing the same comparison as simply testing the difference from chance performance. However, this condition is necessary to ensure that nothing about the task or the stimulus items pull children away from chance responding even when they are only given the opportunity to guess.

VI. GENERAL DISCUSSION

The purpose of the work presented in this monograph is to explore one mechanism of cognitive development that has been largely over-looked—children's ability to recruit information by asking questions. The model presented here proposes that as children explore the world and encounter "problems"—gaps in their knowledge, inconsistencies between their current conceptual structures, and incoming information, or ambiguous information that they are not sure how to process—they can resolve this disequilibrium by asking questions of a more knowledgeable individual. This allows children to gather the information they need precisely when they are ready for it, when they have their conceptual structures up and ready to engage with it. The response they receive can guide their thinking in the right direction, obviating the need for endless trial-and-error hypothesis testing, and can allow the children to make optimal use of the processes they bring to exploring the world around them. Asking these questions, and getting the answers, is an effective tool that allows children to accumulate information as well as reorganize their conceptual structures as they work toward an adult-like understanding of the world.

Before now, there wasn't very much known about the questions children ask—how many they ask, what they ask about, or what relation these questions might have to their cognitive development. The work presented in this monograph presents evidence for the existence and effectiveness of an Information-Requesting Mechanism used by children to learn about the world. Specifically, evidence on five predictions has been presented:

(1) Children can and do ask questions to gather information.

(2) Children get the information they request.

(3) Children are motivated to get the information they request.

(4) The questions children ask are relevant to their cognitive development.

(5) Children can generate questions purposefully to achieve a goal, and use the information they get to reach that goal and achieve a change in knowledge state.

Each of these points will now be taken up in turn.

CHILDREN CAN AND DO ASK QUESTIONS TO GATHER INFORMATION

Children ask questions for a number of purposes, some of which gather information that may not be useful for cognitive development, such as questions that ask for permission ("Can I eat this?"), or clarification ("What did you say?"), among others. Only questions that seek out information ("What is that called?", "Why do dogs bark?") are of potential use for cognitive development; so these are the questions examined in this *Monograph*. The research reported here found that children ask a large number of information-seeking questions, on average 76–95 per hour when engaged in conversation with an adult (or as many as three questions every 2 minutes); over the course of development this would amount to a huge amount of information requested. Asking questions is not something that children do now and then; it is something that is absolutely central to their daily interactions with other people. Study 2 found that this is true even of children who do not yet ask verbal questions. Children as young as 1;0 were able to recruit information from their parents using questioning gestures, expressions, and vocalizations; parents and research assistants were able to reliably interpret these behaviors as requesting certain types of information. So, the ability to gather information that helps them learn about the world from other people is a tool that children have at their disposal from very early on.

Studies 1–3 each report that information-seeking questions constitute the majority of the questions children ask. So, children are not just using questions to ask for permission, clarification, and other such purposes; this tells us that the primary function of questions for children is to support their exploration of their world, and as such these questions potentially constitute a tool that helps propel cognitive development. This is true for the children from 1;0, the earliest age studied.

CHILDREN GET THE INFORMATION THEY REQUEST

Studies 1 and 3 found that children overwhelmingly receive informative answers to their questions. They are significantly more likely to get an answer to their questions than not, and they get the information they ask for as much as 86% of the time. This tells us that parents interpret these questions as serious requests for information, and give the target information to the children. So, from very early on, this mechanism is effectively eliciting information from others, gathering information about the world.

On top of this, parents give additional information that supplements the information children request; as much as 24% of their responses contain such information. This is particularly true when children are at the youngest ages; this information may be complementing the younger children's more limited ability to identify the specific information needed to fully understand the situation at hand. For example, when a child asks "What's mom doing?", if the father were to say "She's shivering," this would answer the child's question, but not get to the heart of the matter; by saying "She's shivering, she's cold," the father tells the child that the activity really is not what is key here, it is his mother's internal state that is important. If the child does not know what a poodle is and asks "What's that?", if the parent answers "it's a poodle," this would answer the question; but the answer "It's a poodle. Poodles are a kind of dog" gives the child a bit of extra help in setting up the proper animal hierarchies. So, children's questions open the door for targeted input from the parents that helps guide their children's thinking in the right direction at precisely the moment they need and want it.

This brings up an important point regarding what constitutes a "good" or an "interesting" question. Graesser and Olde (2003) imply that the "shallow" questions ("fact" questions) asked by adults are not as useful or as "good" as the "deep" questions ("explanatory" questions).[8] Similarly, Miyake and Norman (1979) have made related arguments that a learner has to know what question should be asked in order to ask a good question; in other words, they have to know what they do not know, otherwise they will be unable to generate a useful question. However, as the examples above show, these points may not necessarily be the case, particularly with children. Children need to learn both basic facts about a category/concept/domain, and also underlying core explanatory principles about that category/concept/domain; one without the other is not fully useful. A child (as a very inexperienced learner) learning about how a lock works might have to ask what each of the lock parts are called before being able to move on to questions about how these parts function together. Both of these questions, however, are "good" questions, in that they both serve to get the learner information that they need to take the next step in the learning process. All of these pieces of information are equally valuable to building up an area of knowledge, whether it be understanding biology or understanding how a lock works. Similarly, if a child is faced with a completely bewildering situation, they may not know the proper question to ask, but a simple "what's that" or "why?" might be enough to elicit information from the parent who can walk them through what is going on. Further, the child may have made an incorrect determination about a situation (as in the example of the boy who asked if only naughty people are buried) and may actually ask the *wrong* question; this question still effectively allows the child to get guidance from the adult regarding how to think about these things. From this perspective, then, any question that gets needed information, no matter how imprecisely formed, would be a "good" question, and the learner need not have any conceptual understanding of the topic at hand at all to begin to gather information about the topic.

In fact, this is an important theoretical strength of questions in a nutshell—children need only know that something is confusing or that they are missing some information in order to ask the question, and once the question is asked, the adults who know what is relevant to the situation can guide the child appropriately. This guides revision of the children's knowledge structures, telling them how they should be thinking about the topic at hand. This facilitates learning by obviating endless hypothesis testing, and speeds up learning. Further, this may be especially valuable when it comes to information that might be difficult or impossible for children to learn on their own; this is most clear in cases of largely culturally constructed knowledge, such as a community's religious beliefs. Future research should investigate the role of questions in these cases.

CHILDREN ARE MOTIVATED TO GET THE INFORMATION THEY REQUEST

Studies 1 and 3 found that on the occasions when children do not get the information they requested, they persist in asking for it. They are not satisfied with simply getting any response from the parent; they keep asking until they get the information they asked for, and stop once they get it. So, children's questions are not simply due to an empty attempt to get attention, to attempt to engage in dialogue, or a love of hearing themselves talk (although certainly these priorities show up now and then!). Overall, the purpose of question asking is a genuine attempt to gather information; children want to know the answers to the questions they ask, they know when they've received those answers, and they continue to pursue them if they haven't received them. This is true of the youngest children in these studies; so from the start, children are asking questions with the intention of getting the information they request.

QUESTIONS CHILDREN ASK ARE RELEVANT TO THEIR COGNITIVE DEVELOPMENT

While the ability to recruit information successfully by asking questions is present from the earliest age and thus the mechanism itself does not change, the type of information that children seek out changes to reflect the issues we know them to be working out during the preschool years. This is true both with respect to general question type (fact vs. explanatory information) and specific content.

With respect to general question type, Studies 1–3 all found that children's questions follow the sort of learning progression we would predict from models of question asking during learning tasks with adults. Children's questions show the same shift from asking for facts to asking for more explanatory information that build on the facts and integrate them. This shift occurs generally over time, with explanatory information playing a larger role as children get older; as they get older, they are gathering more explanatory information about the domains they have been learning about. This seems to be especially true between the ages of approximately 3–4 years, when we see a spike in the number of explanatory questions that children ask; this seems to indicate that children go through a period where they are particularly interested in explanatory information. We also see this shift in the short term within a given exchange on a topic. As a child asks a series of several questions on a topic, the probability that a question asks for explanatory information increases as children ask more questions about the topic. So, the questions that children are asking so copiously about the world follow the same progression that adult learner's take as they build up information and become more expert about a topic, evidence that these questions are correspondingly building up information for the children.

Note that these data are neutral with respect to controversies in the cognitive development literature regarding whether or not learning takes place via enrichment or radical reorganization. The position of this paper is that when children encounter disequilibrium in the form of missing or confusing information, they can ask questions which then give them the information they need, and the information they get in response can directly guide the revision of knowledge structures in a targeted way. This could lead to either enrichment or to conceptual reorganization, depending on the question asked and the answer given. In complicated areas of knowledge, this likely takes place over many steps and much time, and over many questions as the child works through different presuppositions and types of evidence.

The specific content that children ask about also changes in ways that parallel the course of cognitive advances we know them to be making. Studies 1 and 2 found that at the time when we know children to be particularly interested in categorizing the world, they ask a large number of label questions, and these questions drop off significantly over time when this is less of a concern for children, showing a parallel between the type of questions being asked at this age and a cognitive advance we know them to be working on. If we manipulate the situation such that many of the objects are novel to the child, and thus they again are faced with a set of objects they need to categorize (as with the animal stimuli in Study 3), questions about labels stay high, showing a flexibility in question-asking that deals with the needs of the current situation. Studies 1–3 also found that Theory of Mind (ToM) questions also parallel children's advances in the area of ToM. At younger ages, when children's ToM is relatively undeveloped, children ask very few questions about ToM. However, as they get older, at the times when we know them to be puzzling out these issues, their questions about ToM increase significantly.

Study 3 was designed to focus on specific stimuli, and examined the questions children ask about one particular topic, animals. Children will begin to start making conceptual developments in the domain of naïve biology between the ages of 4–10; in accord with this, we would expect to see questions about this domain just before and at this age. While children at all ages in this study asked significantly more questions about biological phenomena than they did in study 1, this was particularly true of 3- and 4-year-old children; also, these children were significantly more likely to ask explanatory questions about biological phenomena than about other sorts of phenomena when looking at animals, and this again increases dramatically with age. Children increasingly ask questions such as these about biological phenomena:

(1) Parent: He's eating they're eating their vegetables, huh?
   Child: So they grow?

and increasingly gather information via answers like these, information that may is potentially of use in making advances in understanding biological phenomena:

(2) Child: Why? [Did the crawfish die?]
   Parent: Well maybe he's old.

This change in specific focus on explanatory information within this domain comes just before important conceptual shifts that children will begin to make around and after the age of 4 regarding the life cycle, principles of inheritance, and other biological phenomena.

It is important to stress again that we have no direct evidence in this study to suggest that these questions are responsible for children's upcoming conceptual advances. However, while these data do not demonstrate causality directly, the ages of these children were chosen to look at what is happening just before the conceptual shifts in this domain are occurring; thus, we do have evidence of temporal contiguity with respect to these phenomena that suggest the questions come before the conceptual change. But such evidence is of limited use, and future studies should extend these findings.

103

Study 3's goal of investigating children's questions under more focused conditions also looked at how children's questions change as a result of dealing with different types of stimulus materials, because children may learn differently from different sorts of items. Particularly in the case of biological knowledge, important information, and cues may be lost when we use stimuli other than real animals. The prediction was confirmed; children who saw drawings or three-dimensional replicas of objects asked fewer questions about biological information, and of these reduced questions, there was a further reduction in the number of explanatory questions asked. This decrease was most dramatic in 4-year-olds, the age closest to when the important conceptual shifts begin to occur, and where we see the most explanatory questions about animals being asked in the real animal condition.

This has important implications for teaching and research, both of which predominantly use drawings and replicas. Children are clearly engaged differently with real objects than with drawings or replicas, asking quantitatively more questions about biological phenomena; but not only is there a quantitative difference, there is a qualitative one as well—the kinds of things that interest the children (and thus that they are learning about) are changing with these different items. Different stimuli engage children in different ways, and lead them to ask very different questions. While real animals are avoided in teaching and research for obvious reasons, it is important to realize that something different is happening in the minds of children when they look at these different types of stimuli, and this may have an impact on some aspects of the objects that are highly relevant to the information that is being lost. We should address this where we can. This may be particularly true in the case of research, where we are drawing conclusions about what children do and do not know about biological phenomena, phenomena that may be related to the rich set of contextual cues being lost in pictures or replicas, on the basis of these kinds of stimuli.

Over these three studies, then, the questions children are asking are potentially relevant to the cognitive advances they are making, and change in a way that seems to parallel those advances. While causality cannot be determined by Studies 1–3, even with the evidence of temporal contiguity in Study 3, we can at the least say that the questions are gathering information that has the potential to help children learn about these areas, pending evidence of causality.

CHILDREN CAN GENERATE QUESTIONS PURPOSEFULLY TO ACHIEVE A GOAL AND ACHIEVE A CHANGE IN KNOWLEDGE STATE

Study 4 explores the causal direction of these phenomena; are questions just some knee-jerk reflection of what children are thinking about, or are they gathering targeted information for some purpose? The model presented in this monograph argues that when children encounter a "problem" such as a piece of information they do not know, questions are a tool they can use to get that information, and once they have that information, their knowledge state is changed, and they can now solve the issue at hand.

Study 4 presents evidence that this process does occur in children. When faced with information they need but don't have, children are able to search their existing conceptual knowledge and generate good questions that recruit the needed information; this information changes their knowledge state (they now know what is in the box), and they are then able to employ that information to solve the problem at hand, giving measurable evidence of this change in knowledge state. While there are many ways they can fail at doing this, they are overwhelmingly proficient at the task.

Children first rely on their conceptual structures to generate a question based on what they know about the concepts at hand. Because children do not start off with the less effortful, faster strategy of using perceptual features, this tells us that it is a natural part of the process of asking questions for children to use what they know and apply it to the current situation; this is a default when solving problems that face them. When that conceptual knowledge is pushed to its limits and/or they get fatigued, however, children are able to adapt and find something in the situation that allows them to gather the information they need. Thus, children's ability to use questions to gather the information needed to address some problem facing them is flexible, and adapts to the current situation; children use their existing knowledge when they can, and find alternate methods when that fails them. This flexibility is a particularly useful aspect of the IRM; it allows children to gather information about whatever situation is at hand, even if they don't quite know what it is that they don't know.

So, Study 4 provides evidence that children can formulate useful questions to gather information they need, process the information they recruit, and employ their changed knowledge state effectively. Studies 1 and 3 found that children ask questions persistently until they get the information they have asked for. Together these findings strongly suggest that the questions we see in Studies 1–3 are not cognitively empty reactions to situations, where the child asks a question not for information, but more as a comment on a situation (in effect gathering information by "accident"), and it argues against the possibility that children cannot or do not make use of the information they are requesting. Rather, the findings from these studies argue that these questions have a purposeful component, and gather information that children use effectively. Data reported in Chouinard (2007) further support this; this study found that that information children receive as the result of a question is better remembered than information they are given unbidden; getting information via asking a question results in greater depth of processing for the targeted information. Children care about the information they are asking for, they use this information, and it makes a measurable difference in terms of processing benefits.

The model presented in this paper argues that disequilibrium motivates the information-seeking questions that children ask. While Studies 1–3 were able to confirm that questions are motivated by a desire for information rather than a desire for attention, it proved impossible to separate out what different causes of disequilibrium (gaps in knowledge, ambiguity, etc.) might be responsible for a given question, without knowing each child's history with a given knowledge set. Because of this, the issue of which exact situations motivate questions has to be investigated under more controlled circumstances than naturalistic observation can afford; thus one goal of Study 4 was to create a controlled situation where a certain type of disequilibrium, gaps in knowledge, was created. In this study, children successfully used questions to address these gaps in their knowledge. Future research in this area should expand to explore the ability of children to use questions to address different "problems" (i.e., incomplete knowledge; some contradiction in expectation or knowledge already in place; ambiguous information or circumstances) that potentially lead to disequilibrium. Future studies that explore experimentally how children use questions to resolve ambiguity or conflicting information, for example, would further clarify the range of ways that children effectively use questions. Also, future studies should investigate these issues via procedures that can be used with even younger children, to extend the findings that way, as well.

The model presented in this monograph also argues that while knowledge states can change as a result of a single question, these questions do not necessarily exist in isolation. Many questions, both within an exchange and over time, work together to help children built up information and achieve increasingly more adult-like knowledge structures. So while Study 4 presents evidence of an immediate change in knowledge state as the result of a question, future research should look at how questions are involved in the progressive build-up and change of knowledge states over multiple questions.

CONCLUDING COMMENTS

Together these studies present findings that the skills that are central components of the Information-Requesting Mechanism (IRM) are present from the children's earliest ages, even in 1-year-olds who ask questions via nonverbal means. From very early on, children are able to signal their need for information to adults, and are successful at getting that information from them. The IRM, a tool that allows children to request information in order to effect a change in knowledge state, is in place and is employed from at least 1;0.

While the skills required for the IRM are in place and do not change, children's application of this information-gathering system shifts to recruit information that fits the children's changing needs as their knowledge structures change and become more complex. They gather information that is relevant to the conceptual puzzles the children are currently working out; early on there is a focus on labels, and this drops off with time. As the child gets older, a larger percentage of questions are asking about ToM and biological phenomena. Children can use this tool to get what they need, when they need it.

When research is done in an area that has not had much previous attention, making sure that findings are valid is a very important concern. In this monograph, the studies that investigate the components of children's ability to gather information use very different methodologies. Thus their findings strongly validate one another, and make it unlikely that the result of any given study is an artifact of the methodology employed, or the particular children studied. We can be confident that the patterns reported here document real phenomena.

One important concern that may arise from these data is the generality of the findings, given that all the children studied come from a Western, industrialized culture. In some cultures, and possibly even within different social strata within our own culture, adults do not really converse with children, and so the model presented here arguably might not apply to these children (cf. Ochs & Schieffelin, 1984; Hart & Risely, 1992). Even if parents do not talk to children in these cultures, this would not necessarily invalidate this model; in cultures and social strata such as these, the children still have access to more expert others, usually in the form of older siblings who function as their caretakers. So while this monograph uses the terms "parent" and "adult," this need not be the case; the important dimension with respect to the information source is not that the person be an adult or a parent necessarily, just that they are an appropriate source of more adult-like knowledge than the children themselves already have. Also, the differences between different cultures and social strata are not fully understood yet; for example, Tizard and Hughes (1984) did not find such language differences between the middle-class and working-class children in their study. Future research should extend the findings reported here to other cultures and other strata of our own culture, to better understand what differences exist, and how these differences impact the model presented here.

Related to this is the fact that in three of the four studies here, children were asking questions primarily of their parents. However, many children of these ages also spend a large portion of their day in other settings, interacting with other adults. Tizard and Hughes (1984) found that the same children speak very differently with their parents at home than they do with their teachers at preschool; specifically, children interact more with their parents than with their teachers. So, even with the same child, conversational interactions may vary depending on interlocutor, and thus the data presented here may not be representative of children's interactions with different individuals. Future research should look at how children's questions change when children interact with different people throughout their day.

In addition to the findings reported directly here, this monograph has hinted that questions may be a useful diagnostic tool for investigators. Looking at the content of children's questions may allow us to measure current conceptual structures, and give insight into the issues they are currently puzzling out. Hand-in-hand with this, we may be able to gather evidence about their current conceptual states; for example, children's consistent rate of asking ToM questions when asking about animals suggests that they already consider animals to be beings that have thoughts, beliefs, feelings, and the like. Questions truly are windows into the mind—they allow us a sneak peek into what is going on behind those large, innocent eyes. The little boy who asks whether or not only bad people get buried tells us something important about the facts he's gathered, the inductions, deductions, or abductions that he has made from those facts, and the conclusions he has come to. If this question is anything to go by, systematic exploration of the questions that children ask, in both naturalistic and controlled investigations, promises us a wealth of insight. And of course, this is not coincidental to the fact that these questions are windows that open important opportunities for parents and teachers to give children the information they need.

Taken together, these findings contribute important information about a too-long neglected process that plays an important role in cognitive development. Children are skilled at recruiting needed information from the very start of their ability to communicate with parents; the primary purpose of their question-asking behaviors is to gather information, and they are skilled at generating efficient questions that allow them to solve the problems that face them. Asking questions allows children to move effectively toward adult-like understandings of the world.

NOTE

8. In the context of their study this is true, because the shallow questions do not actually help the learners to solve the problem at hand. So, this is not meant as a criticism of the study, but as a point for larger discussion.

REFERENCES

Benedict, H. (1979). Early lexical development: Comprehension and production. *Journal of Child Language*, **6**, 183–200.

Berlyne, D., & Frommer, F. (1966). Some determinants of the incidence and content of children's questions. *Child Development*, **37** (1), 177–189.

Blank, S., & Covington, M. (1965). Inducing children to ask questions in solving problems. *The Journal of Educational Research*, **59** (1), 21–27.

Bobrow, D. G., & Bower, G. H. (1969). Comprehension and recall of sentences. *Journal of Experimental Psychology*, **80**, 455–461.

Bower, G. H., & Clark, M. C. (1969). Narrative stories as mediators for serial learning. *Psychonomic Science*, **14**, 181–182.

Bransford, J. D., & Johnson, M. K. (1972). Contextual prerequisites for understanding: Some investigations of comprehension and recall. *Journal of Verbal Learning and Verbal Behavior*, **11**, 717–726.

Burns, D. J. (1992). The consequences of generation. *Journal of Memory and Language*, **31**, 615–633.

Callanan, M., & Oakes, L. (1992). Preschoolers' questions and parents' explanations: Causal thinking in everyday activity. *Cognitive Development*, **7**, 213–233.

Campos, J. J., & Stenberg, C. R. (1981). Perception, appraisal, and emotion: The onset of social referencing. In M. E. Lamb & L. R. Sherrod (Eds.), *Infants' social cognition: Empirical and social considerations* (pp. 273–314). Hillsdale, NJ: Erlbaum.

Carey, S. (1985). *Conceptual change in childhood*. Cambridge, MA: MIT Press.

Carey, S. (1999). Sources of conceptual change. In E. K. Scholnick & K. Nelson et al. (Eds.), *Conceptual development: Piaget's legacy* (pp. 293–326). Mahway, NJ, USA: Lawrence Erlbaum Associates, Inc.

Chouinard, M. M. (2007). *The benefits of asking: Recruiting information results in greater recall*. Manuscript under review.

Craik, F. I. M., & Lockhart, R. S. (1972). Levels of processing: A framework for memory research. *Journal of Verbal Learning and Verbal Behavior*, **11**, 671–684.

Dallett, K. M. (1964). Number of categories and category information in free recall. *Journal of Experimental Psychology*, **68**, 1–12.

Eiser, C. (1976). Questions children ask about spatial arrays: An analysis of the processes involved in coordinating perspectives. *British Journal of Educational Psychology*, **46**, 203–211.

Flavell, J. (1999). Cognitive development: Children's knowledge about the mind. *Annual Review of Psychology*, **50**, 21–45.

Flavell, J., Green, F., & Flavell, E. (1995). Young children's knowledge about thinking. *Monographs of the Society for Research in Child Development*, **60** (1), 243.

Goldfield, B. A., & Reznick, J. S. (1990). Early lexical acquisition: Rate, content, and the vocabulary spurt. *Journal of Child Language*, **17**, 171–184.

Gopnik, A., & Astington, J. W. (1988). Children's understanding of representational change and its relation to the understanding of false belief and the appearance-reality distinction. *Child Development*, **59**, 26–37.

Gopnik, A., & Meltzoff, A. (1997). *Words, thoughts and theories*. Cambridge, MA: MIT Press.

Gopnik, A., Meltzoff, A. N., & Kuhl, P. K. (1999). *The scientist in the crib: Minds, brains, and how children learn*. Cambridge, MA: MIT Press.

Gopnik, A., & Wellman, H. M. (1994). The theory theory. In L. Hirschfeld & S. A. Gelman (Eds.), *Mapping the mind: Domain specificity in cognition and culture* (pp. 257–293). New York: Cambridge University Press.

Graesser, A. C., & McMahen, C. L. (1993). Anomalous information triggers questions when adults solve quantitative problems and comprehend stories. *Journal of Educational Psychology*, **85** (1), 136–151.

Graesser, A. C., & Olde, B. A. (2003). How does one know whether a person understands a device? The quality of the questions the person asks when the device breaks down. *Journal of Educational Psychology*, **95** (3), 524–536.

Harris, P. (2000). On not falling down to earth. In K. S. Rosengren, C. N. Johnson & P. L. Harris (Eds.), *Imagining the impossible* (pp. 157–177). Cambridge: Cambridge University Press.

Hart, B., & Risely, T. (1992). American parenting of language-learning children: Persisting differences in family-child interactions observed in natural home environments. *Developmental Psychology*, **28** (6), 1096–1105.

Hirschman, E., & Bjork, R. A. (1988). The generation effect: Support for a two-factor theory. *Journal of Experimental Psychology: Learning, Memory, and Cognition*, **14**, 484–494.

Ironsmith, M., & Whitehurst, G. (1978). The development of listener abilities in communication: How children deal with ambiguous information. *Child Development*, **49**, 348–352.

Isaacs, N. (1930). Children's "why" questions. In S. Isaacs (Ed.), *Intellectual growth in young children* (pp. 291–349). London: Routledge (Appendix A).

Jaakkola, R., & Slaughter, V. (2002). Children's body knowledge: Understanding "life" as a biological goal. *British Journal of Developmental Psychology*, **20**, 325–342.

Johnson, S., & Solomon, G. (1997). Why dogs have puppies and cats have kittens: The role of birth in young children's understanding of biological origins. *Child Development*, **68** (3), 404–419.

Kenyon, B. (2001). Current research in children's conceptions of death: A critical review. *Omega*, **43** (1), 63–91.

Kirkham, N., Cruess, L., & Diamond, A. (2003). Helping children apply their knowledge to their behavior on a dimension-switching task. *Developmental Science*, **6** (5), 449–476.

MacWhinney, B., & Snow, C. E. (1985). The Child Language Data Exchange System (CHILDES). *Journal of Child Language*, **12**, 271–294.

Markman, E. (1977). Realizing that you don't understand: A preliminary investigation. *Child Development*, **48**, 986–992.

Markman, E. (1979). Realizing that you don't understand: Elementary school children's awareness of inconsistencies. *Child Development*, **50**, 643–655.

Meltzoff, A. N. (1988a). Infant imitation after a 1-week delay: Long-term memory for novel acts and multiple stimuli. *Developmental Psychology*, **24**, 470–476.

Meltzoff, A. N. (1988b). Infant imitation and memory: Nine-month-olds in immediate and deferred tests. *Child Development*, **59**, 217–225.

Meltzoff, A. N. (1990). Foundations for developing a concept of self: The role of imitation in relating self to other and the value of social mirroring, social modeling, and self practice in infancy. In D. Cicchetti & M. Beeghly (Eds.), *The self in transition: Infancy to childhood* (pp. 139–167). Chicago: University of Chicago Press.

Miyake, N., & Norman, D. (1979). To ask a question, one must know enough to know what is not known. *Journal of Verbal Learning and Verbal Behavior,* **18**, 357–364.

Ochs, E., & Schieffelin, B. (1984). Language acquisition and socialization: Three developmental stories. In R. Schweder & R. Levin (Eds.), *Culture theory: Essays in mind, self and emotion* (pp. 276–320). New York: Cambridge University Press.

Piaget, J. (1926). *The language and thought of the child.* New York: Harcourt Brace.

Piaget, J. (1954). *The construction of reality in the child.* New York: Ballantine books.

Rosengren, K., Gelman, S., Kalish, C., & McCormick, M. (1991). As time goes by: Children's early understanding of growth in animals. *Child Development,* **62** (6), 1302–1320.

Ross, H. S., & Killey, J. C. (1977). The effect of questioning on retention. *Child Development,* **48**, 312–314.

Scardamalia, M., & Bereiter, C. (1992). Text-based and Knowledge-based questioning by children. *Cognition and Instruction,* **9** (3), 177–199.

Schank, R. C. (1986). *Explanations patterns: Understanding mechanically and creatively.* Hillsdale, NJ: Erlbaum.

Schwabe, A. M., Olswang, L. B., & Kriegsmann, E. (1986). Requests for information: Linguistic, cognitive, pragmatic, and environmental variables. *Language, Speech, and Hearing Services in Schools,* **17**, 38–55.

Siegal, M. (1988). Children's knowledge of contagion and contamination as causes of illness. *Child Development,* **59** (5), 1353–1359.

Solomon, G. (2002). Birth, kind, and naïve biology. *Developmental Science,* **5** (2), 213–218.

Solomon, G. E. A., & Cassimatis, N. L. (1999). On facts and conceptual systems: Young children's integration of their understanding of germs and contagion. *Developmental Psychology,* **35** (1), 113–126.

Solomon, G., Johnson, S., Zaitchick, D., & Carey, S. (1996). Like father, like son: Young children's understanding of how and why offspring resemble their parents. *Child Development,* **67** (1), 151–171.

Springer, K., & Keil, F. (1989). On the development of biologically specific beliefs: The case of inheritance. *Child Development,* **60** (3), 637–648.

Sully, J. (1896). *Studies of childhood.* New York: D. Appleton and Company.

Tizard, B., & Hughes, M. (1984). *Young children learning.* Cambridge, MA: Harvard University Press.

Tomasello, M. (1999a). *The cultural origins of human cognition.* Cambridge, MA: Harvard University Press.

Tomasello, M. (1999b). The human adaptation for culture. *Annual Review of Anthropology,* **28**, 509–529.

Vosniadou, S. (1994). Universal and culture-specific properties of children's mental models of the earth. In L. Hirschfeld & S. Gelman (Eds.), *Mapping the mind* (pp. 412–430). Cambridge: Cambridge University Press.

Vygotsky, L. (1978). *Mind in society: The development of higher psychological processes.* Cambridge: Harvard University Press.

Zelazo, P. D., Frye, D., & Rapus, T. (1996). An age-related dissociation between knowing rules and using them. *Cognitive Development,* **11** (1), 37–63.

ACKNOWLEDGMENTS

This research was supported in part by research grants from the National Institute of Health.

I thank Eve Clark, Herb Clark, John Flavell, Natasha Kirkham, and Michael Ramscar for invaluable advice and for providing constructive comments on a previous version of this article. I also thank the anonymous reviewers for their valuable advice regarding previous versions of this manuscript. I also thank Lera Boroditsky and Anne Fernald for extremely helpful discussions regarding the work.

This work would not have been possible without the help of the parents, children, and staff of Bing Nursery school, who generously gave their time and trust. It also would not be possible without a hard-working team of research assistants, including Brooke Alexander, Brenda Bantados, Katy Blakemore, Adryon Burton, Serina Chang, Christina Davis, Lupe Flores, Jennifer Heil, Salima Mussani, Philip Rowe, and Marie White. Assistants who played a smaller, but nonetheless crucial role include Brian Cabral, Dawn Felton, Manching Harriman, Katie Heaton, Kristi Imberi, Wendy Jaskowiak, Lisa Matthews, and Sabrina Mishra.

Correspondence concerning this article should be addressed to Dr. Michelle M. Chouinard, Department of SSHA, University of California, Merced, PO Box 2039, Merced, CA 95344. E-mail: mchouinard@ucmerced.edu.

TIME FOR QUESTIONS

Paul L. Harris

Michelle Chouinard has written a lucid, persuasive monograph. The four studies, relatively diverse in their methodology, drive home the point that children—even when they are toddlers—seek information via questions, generally receive informative answers, and persist with their questions when they do not.

The study of children's questions has been conducted intermittently for more than a century. The endeavor reaches back to one of the earliest writers on child psychology, James Sully, who analyzed the questions posed by his son (Sully, 2000 [1896]). Chouinard's monograph is a welcome advance for two reasons. First, previous analyses typically focused on selected questions noted down by investigators. By contrast, Chouinard's analysis of data gathered via CHILDES means that we now have a much more comprehensive and representative picture of the frequency and content of children's questions. Second, Chouinard's theoretical approach coincides with a growing appreciation of the ways in which children might learn from what other people say to them (Gelman, 2003; Harris & Koenig, 2006). As Chouinard points out, previous writers were inclined to treat children's questions as an index of their preexisting ideas. They did not dwell on the possibility that questions might serve as an engine for cognitive development.

In thinking about the larger implications of Chouinard's monograph for future research, I comment on four issues: the identity of the child's conversation partner; social class variation in the frequency and persistence of children's questions; the way that children respond to answers to their questions; and the cognitive impact of answering children's questions.

THE IDENTITY OF THE CHILD'S CONVERSATION PARTNER

In three of the four studies, children were mostly, if not always, talking to their parents. In this connection, it is appropriate to cite an earlier monograph by Barbara Tizard and Martin Hughes—*Young Children Learning*. Having recorded the conversations of 4-year-old girls both at home and at preschool, Tizard and Hughes (1984) found that sustained and tenacious question of an adult—what they called "passages of intellectual search"—occurred rarely, if ever, in preschool but were fairly common at home with the mother. These authors anticipate some of the conclusions of Chouinard's monograph, particularly her emphasis on questions as a key mechanism for cognitive development, but they also highlight the possibility that there may be something special about parent–child dialogue. Admittedly, Chouinard reports that questions were also frequent and well formed in Study 4 when children were interacting with an experimenter rather than a parent. However, to play the game in Study 4, children had little option but to pose questions so that the findings are scarcely an index of children's natural mode of conversation with adults who are not their parents.

Why might children ask more questions of a parent? Two different factors come to mind. First, it is easier—and more appropriate—for children to monopolize the attention of a parent as compared to a teacher. Beyond such contextual or pragmatic factors, however, it is also intuitively plausible that deep-seated interpersonal factors are at work. In developmental psychology, we have long accepted the idea that children regard certain adults as emotionally available and form an affective attachment to them. My guess is that young children also come to regard certain adults as intellectually available and form an epistemic attachment to them. Stated differently, when children seek information, they are likely to be selective in whom they question and whose answers they assimilate, just as when they make a bid for emotional reassurance, they are selective in whom they approach and whose gestures of comfort they accept. It remains an open question how far these two types of relationship coincide. Children who have a secure emotional attachment to a parent might be thereby more inclined to question him or her in a trusting or sustained fashion. However, it is also possible that attachment security, as traditionally conceived, bears little relationship to the kind of epistemic trust that I have in mind. Instead, such trust might depend on the cognitive stance that is taken by particular interlocutors. One way to throw light on this issue would be to replicate the type of investigation that Tizard and Hughes conducted (i.e., systematic recording of conversations between parent and child in the home setting) but to include an examination of the effect of attachment status on the frequency and diligence with which children ask questions of their parents. Such an investigation could indicate the extent to which attachment status or alternatively the cognitive stance of the parent—or both—predict individual differences among children in their questioning of a given adult. In the next section, I pursue in more detail the issue of how a parent's cognitive stance might influence the way that a child asks questions.

CLASS MATTERS

Michelle Chouinard's brisk introduction could leave the impression that hers is the first systematic study of children's questions. Yet this is not quite true. Indeed, in their attention to social class difference, some earlier studies were more systematic. For example, in 1930, Dorothea McCarthy reported a study of 140 children in Minneapolis ranging from 18 to 54 months. Children's first 50 utterances were recorded as they each interacted with the same adult. A notable finding, especially given such relatively well-controlled conditions, was that a greater proportion of those 50 utterances were questions among upper-class children as compared to lower-class children. This class difference was quite evident at 24–30 months and was still apparent at 48–54 months. McCarthy (1930) went on to examine such differences while controlling for mental age. Even with this precaution, a robust social class difference emerged. For example, among upper-class children with a mental age of 48–54 months, almost 20% of their utterances were in the form of a question. By contrast, among lower-class children with a mental age of 48–54 months less that 10% were in the form of question.

Some of this variation might be attributable to the greater confidence of upper-class children in posing questions to a stranger—all children had been invited to interact with the same, relatively unfamiliar adult. However, a similar class difference emerged some 50 years later in the U.K. study mentioned earlier by Tizard and Hughes (1984) in which children were recorded in conversation with their mothers. Although the overall proportion of conversation turns devoted to questions was only slightly greater for middle- as compared with working-class children, middle-class children asked more curiosity-based questions as opposed to questions that focused on procedural matters or challenged parental authority (Tizard & Hughes, 1984, p. 150).[1]

Recall that Tizard and Hughes observed the same children both at home and at preschool. Despite the fact that all children, irrespective of social class, asked many fewer questions at preschool (about two per hour) as compared with home (about 26 per hour) and virtually never engaged in passages of intellectual search at preschool, this dramatic reduction in the frequency and persistence of children's questions did not eliminate class differences. Whereas middle-class children mainly asked curiosity-based questions at preschool, working-class children mainly asked procedural questions.

Why did the middle-class children ask more questions, especially curiosity-based questions, in both settings? One possibility is that they had become used to receiving informative replies at home. Certainly, middle-class mothers were more likely to say that they enjoyed answering their children's questions. However, Tizard and Hughes (1984) found no relationship between the frequency of children's questions and the adequacy of the replies that they received. Yet there was a link to the mothers' own conversational style. Mothers who asked more questions had children who asked more questions.

Hart and Risley (1992) reported further suggestive evidence on this potential causal link. They conducted a longitudinal study of parent–child interaction in the homes of 40 children, representing the range of American families in terms of socioeconomic status. On average, one-third of parental utterances were questions—and this percentage remained quite stable for children ranging from 10–36 months. Nevertheless, there was considerable variation in that percentage across families—from <20% to almost 50%—and that variation remained stable over the 27-month period during which observations were conducted. Hart and Risley (1992) found that the frequency of questioning by parents was positively related to their tendency to take up, repeat, or expand upon what their child had just said but negatively related to the tendency to issue prohibitions such as: "stop" or "don't (do that)." Thus, it appears that parents vary in the frequency with which they treat conversation as a mode of intellectual exploration and elaboration. We may plausibly speculate that parents who model that cognitive stance in their conversation are more likely to have children who emulate it.

In sum, Michelle Chouinard has likely identified a universal mechanism by which children gather information. Nonetheless, upper- and middle-class parents ask questions more often than lower class parents and their children reproduce this pattern. These class differences are carried over into the school setting. Even if questions serve the same information-seeking function for all children, the extent to which that function is exercised varies by class. Further research on individual and class differences should help us to understand how this mechanism is nurtured.

PASSAGES OF INTELLECTUAL SEARCH

When children pose a question, particularly a question that calls for an explanation, they may or may not receive a satisfactory answer. As Chouinard emphasizes, children can be relatively tenacious in pursuing an issue. They are much more likely to persist with their questions when adults' replies fail to supply the information they sought. Not only are children tenacious in repeating the same question, they often pose a series of related questions. Thus, from the age of 30 months, more than half of children's questions in Study 1 formed part of a coherent sequence rather than standing in isolation. Requests for explanation were especially likely to be embedded in such a sequence. Children often started by asking for factual information and then moved on to pose explanation-oriented questions.

As mentioned earlier, Tizard and Hughes (1984) also noticed these bouts of tenacious questioning and examined them in some detail. They found that, in general, such a sustained focus on the same topic was fairly unusual among the 4-year-olds that they observed. Less than one-fifth of their conversations at home lasted for 22 turns or more. However, this was true for more than half of their so-called passages of intellectual search. Note, however, that a striking class difference again emerged. Such passages were observed in 87% of the middle-class families as compared with 27% of the working-class families.

Tenacious questioning might show that children will persist until they have acquired the information they need. This formulation suggests that a series of questions is motivated only by the search for some missing piece of information. Chouinard tends to describe children as operating in this fashion: "They keep asking for the information until they receive it, and stop once they do" (p. 46). However, reading the transcripts provided by earlier investigators, one is left with the impression that children's follow-up questions are sometimes intended to qualify, protest, or reject, the information they have been offered. Scrutiny of some examples will indicate what I have in mind.

Sully (1896) reports the following exchange between his wife and their 4-year-old son. Having been told that seals are killed for their skins and for their oil, the boy asked: "Why do they kill the stags? They don't want their skins, do they?" His mother explained: "No, they kill them because they like to chase them."[2] The child asked: "Why don't policemen stop them?" "They can't do that because people are allowed to kill them." The child protested: "Allowed, allowed? People are not allowed to take other people and kill them." His mother countered: "People think there is a difference between killing men and killing animals." Woe-begone, the child answered: "You don't understand me." Such skeptical responding is not confined to children growing up in an academic family. Consider the following exchange reported by Tizard and Hughes (1984). Four-year-old Rosy was puzzled about why a window cleaner was given money. In the course of a long exchange, her mother explained: "Well, the window-cleaner needs money doesn't he?" "Why?" asked Rosy. "To buy clothes for his children and food for them to eat." Rosy objected: "Well, sometimes window-cleaners don't have children." Similarly, when Beth (just under 4 years) was offered an explanation by her mother for why roofs slope: ". . . Otherwise, if you have a flat roof, the rain would sit in the middle of the roof and make a big puddle, and then it would start coming through," she responded: "Our school has a flat roof, you know."

These three examples suggest that when children search for an explanation via conversation, two related processes come into play. They do register the claims that they are offered (animals are killed for their skins; window cleaners need money to feed their children; sloping roofs allow rainwater to drain). Nevertheless, children examine those claims to check how far they cover other known cases. Children may then question apparent anomalies (animals not hunted for their skins; childless window cleaners; buildings with flat roofs). Thus, when children are offered an explanation, they engage in a sifting process. They do not simply stockpile information.

How widespread is such caution? We do not know the answer but Chouinard's careful analysis of the data from CHILDES offers a good starting point. Her coding indicates the frequency with which children do or do not get the information they seek. She reports that children typically desist when they receive an answer and persist when they do not. My guess is that this dichotomy does not capture every interchange. There may be occasions when children are given the information that they asked for but because it does not fully satisfy them or throws up anomalies, they continue to pose questions. Thus, it would be informative to know how often children challenge or seek to qualify claims that adults offer in response to their questions.

In this context, it would also be interesting to probe individual differences. If children frequently engage in passages of intellectual search, does that apparent manifestation of epistemic trust mean that they are especially accepting of what the adult tells them? Alternatively, is the capacity for sustained questioning the hallmark of an intellectually cautious child—someone who actively seeks clarification in the context of dialogue but someone who is also willing to challenge a trusted interlocutor? I speculate further on this issue as follows.

COGNITIVE IMPACT OF ANSWERING CHILDREN'S QUESTIONS

Chouinard understandably focuses on ways in which the *content* of the replies that children receive to their questions might impact their cognitive development. For example, she draws attention to the possibility that children's burgeoning biological knowledge might benefit from answers to their informal queries about what animals eat, how they reproduce, and so forth. In future research, however, I think it will also be important to delve beneath the content of the replies that children receive in order to analyze the implicit epistemology that guides a parent's reply. Such tacit messages are likely to shape children's developing conception of how knowledge is acquired and how secure that knowledge is.

Musing on how to satisfactorily reply to a child who asked: "Why don't we see two things with our two eyes?" Nathan Isaacs (1930, p. 309) approaches this interesting issue in the following way: "The child ... turns to the adult trustfully, ready as a rule to accept whatever he gets as the right help, since offered. Moreover, he must in large measure form his standard of what constitutes right help, i.e. satisfactory explanation, from what he gets from the adult." Pursuing Isaac's comment, it is easy to imagine that parents vary in the solicitude with which they answer questions and the authority or confidence with which they convey those answers. Children who receive comprehensive and confident answers are likely to draw different conclusions about the nature and certainty of knowledge as compared to children who receive answers that are fragmentary or uncertain. More generally, the pattern of answers that children receive to their questions is likely to promote a particular conception of what it is to arrive at an explanation.

In this regard, Isaacs noted an intriguing paradox. Children probably come to discern who supplies them with more or less satisfactory answers to their questions. Indeed such selective trust in informants is already apparent in the preschool years (Clément, Koenig, & Harris, 2004; Jaswal & Neely, 2006; Koenig & Harris, 2005; Koenig, Clément, & Harris, 2004). Yet trust, once established, carries certain risks. Isaacs (1930, p. 314) comments on the child's dilemma in the following way: "One can even say that, up to a point, the more helpful guidance he gets on the whole, the more he may lay himself open to take over any unhelpful leads as well—as if they were one of the forms or degrees of helpfulness, drawn from the superior wisdom of the adult." In other words, the epistemic trust that I invoked earlier may lead children to be insufficiently skeptical of the answers they receive. When parents are obliged to confess ignorance or doubt, they may also serve their child's cognitive development.

CONCLUSIONS

Chouinard's monograph is likely to become a landmark in research on children's questions and their role in cognitive development. Her central claim is that children are well equipped from an early age to seek information from other people by asking questions. That central claim opens up fascinating new questions for research. I have sought to identify four. Do children put their questions to particular people? Does a child's family influence how often and how persistently he or she asks questions? How far do children sift and check the answers they receive? Finally, do those answers shape not just what children know about a given topic but their broader conception of knowledge and its acquisition?

119

NOTES

1. Chouinard (p. 121) writes: "Tizard and Hughes (1984) did not find these language differences between the middle-class and working-class children in their study." This claim is puzzling because Tizard and Hughes actually report several social class differences.

2. Sully's 4-year-old son would find 21st century Britain no more congenial. The stalking and shooting of stags is still legal.

References

Clément, F., Koenig, M., & Harris, P. L. (2004). The ontogenesis of trust in testimony. *Mind and Language*, **19**, 360–379.

Gelman, S. A. (2003). *The essential child*. New York, USA: Oxford University Press.

Harris, P. L., & Koenig, M. (2006). Trust in testimony: How children learn about science and religion. *Child Development*, **77**, 505–524.

Hart, B., & Risley, T. (1992). American parenting of language-learning children: Persisting differences in family-child interactions observed in natural home environments. *Developmental Psychology*, **28**, 1096–1105.

Isaacs, N. (1930). Children's "why" questions. In S. Isaacs (Ed.), *Intellectual growth in young children* (pp. 291–349). London: George Routledge & Sons.

Jaswal, V. K., & Neely, L. A. (2006). Adults don't always know best: Preschoolers use past reliability over age when learning new words. *Psychological Science*, **17**, 757–758.

Koenig, M., Clément, F., & Harris, P. L. (2004). Trust in testimony: Children's use of true and false statements. *Psychological Science*, **10**, 694–698.

Koenig, M., & Harris, P. L. (2005). Preschoolers mistrust ignorant and inaccurate speakers. *Child Development*, **76**, 1261–1277.

McCarthy, D. A. (1930). *The language development of the preschool child*. Minneapolis, MI: University of Minnesota Press.

Sully, J. (2000). *Studies of childhood* (1st ed., 1896.) London: Free Association Books.

Tizard, B., & Hughes, M. (1984). *Young children learning*. London: Fontana.

Michael P. Maratsos

According to that most useful of all sources, someone's office door, Bernard Kaplan once said that progress in psychology often consists of psychologists knocking down obstacles they have previously put up for themselves. Why is this frustrating observation so accurate? Chiefly, the reason is that a gifted figure commonly comes up with a good idea that is, in fact, reasonably true or useful a good deal of the time. But then he seeks to make this good idea cover everything. Humans—and children—being a complicated evolutionary product, this never works; and the new idea, having sought to explain everything, becomes a new obstacle to be knocked down. Unfortunately, its replacement frequently then begins a similar process of expanding the often true into the always true, which sets up a new obstacle.

For the present monograph, the obvious previous obstacle is the odd and striking Avoidance of the Adult that seems so central Piaget's work. His aversion to adult influence on development is pervasive, and so deep as to signal something personal. In his early work, like *Language and Thought of the Child* (Piaget, 1997), Piaget believed that the social world did have beneficial effects on children's development; but this beneficial influence all came from argument and discussion with peers. In summaries written later in his life, he still upheld the importance of social interaction with peers for the child's escape from social egocentrism, though not so much for the child's grappling with logic and mathematics that occupied his later years. But when asked about the obvious fact that children hear a good deal from adults at home or in school, he always just grumbled that this had to be filtered through the child's own cognitive structures—an answer which is true, but also diverts the argument.

It is a little surprising that Piaget had such animus toward social transmission, because he had a keen awareness of how much our view of earth's place in the universe, for example, had changed because of the socially transmitted work of a very few gifted astronomers. Anthropologists' work similarly shows how important cultural transmissions are. Our children believe at a precociously early age in the germ theory of disease, another recent invention of a gifted few. This differs greatly from the belief very common among primitive groups that all serious illnesses and all nonaccidental deaths occur as the result of malevolent sorcery from some outsider, so every such death demands revenge on the relevant person or his tribe. This theory has quite different social ramifications than the Western view, to say the least. Both theories no doubt depended on the efforts of a small number of imaginative individuals. Probably most of what we believe or know past the level of rather basic cognition is a result of social transmissions from our superiors in status and knowledge.

Vygotsky famously sought to reverse Piaget's excess here. Vygotsky was fully committed to Soviet ideals that humans and their development are a product of society. In particular, adults play a crucial role in children's development in using language to transmit knowledge and beliefs to children. It is to Vygotsky's credit that, implicitly, he retained a great deal of Piaget's thinking even while attempting to correct him: Vygotsky's thinking about scaffolding explicitly recognized that the adult's input could only advance in collaboration with the child's own state of knowledge, a very Piagetian idea. But he stressed how the skill and superior knowledge of the adult, who serves as the transmission tool for society in general, offer much that the child alone could not observe or construct. He reasserted, in effect, common sense about these matters.

The Vygotskyan position has become one of the major traditions of current research, and the present monograph appears firmly embedded in the Vygotskyan canon. In the Vygotskyan mode, it proclaims that children gain a good deal of information from adults. A great many parents, furthermore, would no doubt endorse the main conclusions as empirically commonsensical indeed. Children ask a good many questions, about facts and causes among other things. They ask because they want to know and believe adults will be a useful source of information. When they do not get enough of an answer, they keep asking, and when they do, they stop (which indicates it is not just all about getting attention, a very useful observation). I think the work in the monograph establishes that this sensible and not at all trivial conclusion applies extremely well to a wide group of children. Furthermore, I think the analytic skill with which these matters were checked out makes them completely believable.

This is all so reasonable that one might ask why it took this long for this work to appear. While there are always many reasons for such things, I think part of the reason is theoretical: we like our ideas to fall completely within one distinctive theoretical orientation, but these findings fall into two theoretical orientations at once, not just one. At first glance, as I said above, the work seems clearly to fall in the Vygotskyan canon. But in fact, I think closer inspection shows this is not completely true. Vygotsky certainly was interested in what adults could give to children. But his belief in the importance of social influence did not incline him to think of the child as an active, self-motivated seeker after knowledge and cognitive growth; this idea was more central in Piaget. Vygotsky's world is one of helpful, initiatory adults, not one of active, initiatory children.

The children of this monograph thus do not quite fit into the thought of either of these two great theorists and world-builders. The children do get a lot of information from helpful adults, who try to give information that will be useful—adults out of the happy part of Vygotsky's world. But they are active in seeking the information, which is out of Piaget's world, not really Vygotsky's. To complicate matters further, though they seek the information actively, they do not give the impression that they try to figure out everything themselves first, unlike the leaning-to-autonomy Piagetian child. They probably recur rather easily to just asking about animals, instead of, say, observing them carefully for 10 minutes or an hour, before they finally seek adult help. They are probably, in fact, a little bit lazy, according to Piagetian standards; they are certainly not as independent as his ideal child.

Personally I think these children are quite real and understandable. Our great theorists, as usual, driven by some personal vision of the way the world works, set up ideas whose purity makes them more appealing, but are in fact incomplete and overextended. We do not need to cooperate with their error by taking it that in any given situation, one or the other of them must be right in opposition to the other. These children do not seem to me interested in being either pure Piagetians or pure Vygotskyans, as I understand these things, but one imagines things are working out for them all right anyway. It is well known in the world of pets that mutts, who are in effect crossbreed hybrids, are actually healthier than purebred animals. I think that in all likelihood, children are theoretical mutts, not purebreds. I think the current monograph, properly understood, does very well to support such a useful hybrid understanding of what children are up to. I believe this mongrel status of the behavior, has been partly responsible for its failing to appear in our annals despite its ecological obviousness.

So far I think we have some straightforward and valuable findings, that illuminate both a specific behavior and a more general lesson—that even a single behavior can be seen as using elements from what seem like opposed theories—which entail radically different views of the child. Past these clearer points, I believe we encounter more uncertain problems, in particular the problem of cultural influence. That is, very clearly this behavior builds on some general traits of children: their early ability and interest, in building what the pragmatics researchers call intersubjectivity, that is a shared social mental and emotional scene with others. Very likely, a certain amount of curiosity as well is widespread and natural in children.

But the anthropological and historical literatures, in which Vygotsky was always keenly interested, also suggest cultural circumstances play a role. From what we currently know, in many groups and cultures, "children should be seen and not heard" is more than a wistful slogan; it is a program of social action. Vygotsky's own work with Luria found Russian peasants to be generally notably uncurious and speculative. These conclusions accord well with what anthropologists and historians have often found in societies, especially in intensive agricultural ones (e.g., Johnson & Earle, 1987), but also with the attitudes of older Western urban societies towards children (e.g., Pollock, 2001).

Current anthropological work with children, both within American society and outside it, lends support. Ochs and Schieffelin (1995) describe a general attitude in Samoan society that children should defer to, and listen to, their elders, including both adults and older siblings, and not put themselves forward in speech or otherwise (see also Ortner, 1981) Indeed, Keith Kernan (1969), trying to get a language sample from Samoan children, was able to record only a handful of multiword utterances over a period of months as a result. Observations of Guatemalan preschool children show similar success (from the adult point of view): the children listen and observe quietly to learn. Tolbert (1978) found that Spanish-speaking children she observed in similar contexts did not speak like American 2-year-olds, until around three; she attributed this to nutritional problems, but it would also follow from this sort of language input. LeVine and LeVine (1981) remark that the African parents they studied sought to avoid close emotional relations with their children, seeking instead obedience. Their speech to the children consisted largely of commands. The children were expected to gain more sociable experience from older siblings and other adults, but we do not know what the nature of the verbal experiences might be.

In the United States, no known methodological problems invalidate Hart and Risley's (1995) findings that a great many working class and poor parents talk rarely with their children; indeed, in their study, the 3-year-old children of the professional group had a larger productive vocabulary than the welfare mothers of their study. Heath's (1983) classic ethnographic studies of different communities in a South Carolina town suggest the same; she found parental use and questioning about labeling to be universal among her middle-class sample, Black or White, but less common or absent among working-class or poor families. The entering classes in many American urban public schools today have an average vocabulary that is at the fifth percentile of the American average (Whitehurst, 2001). Surely these children were not getting to hear and ask about word labels very often. The

COMMENTARY

anthropological literature suggests this kind of situation may not be as deviant as it naturally strikes us.

In our society, in contrast, it is a much more common belief that the acquisition of knowledge and verbal skill are necessary for the maintenance or improvement of social status, and possibly to the development of individual character. The playing of the "original word game," giving and asking for labels, probably comprises part of this orientation.

If these suggestions about cultural influences prove to be correct, they do not show that such questioning behavior is "purely environmental," or even requires intensive modeling to get started. As I remarked above, it surely rests in part on some highly general characteristics of human children. In reading about some of these intensive agricultural societies, one has a clear feeling that there is an active effort, both direct and indirect, to mold children into more obedient, less quiet individuals than they might naturally wish to be; this was certainly true of nonmodern Western societies, from the records we have available. While parts of our society might be seen as actively instigating and encouraging such behavior, perhaps in reality they are just mostly enabling it. These are not such easy questions.

Whatever the answer to the second, difficult set of questions about the relations of biological and environmental discouragement and encouragement, we should be very impressed by the volume and intensity, and intellectually well-structured nature, of question asking documented in this study. This documentation is not just relevant to the conflicts between Piaget and Vygotsky. A good deal of modern "theory" work, for example, follows Piaget in picturing the "important things" as being gotten by the child acting and thinking mostly alone (see, e.g., Gelman & Opfer, 2004; Wellman & Gelman, 1998) a new reinstatement of the Piagetian "lone investigator." In fact, the children of this study seem quite happy to enlist the aid of others about such matters. I think we need to realize, once again, that our theories desire more theoretical and emotional metaphorical self-consistency in all these matters than our rather pragmatic children do.

References

Brown, R. (1973). *A first language*. Cambridge, MA: Harvard University Press.
Gelman, S., & Opfer, J. E. (2004). The development of the animate-inanimate distinction. In U. Goswami (Ed.), *The handbook of child cognitive development* (pp. 151–166). Oxford: Blackwell.
Hart, B., & Risley, T. R. (1995). *Meaningful differences in the everyday experience of young American children*. Baltimore: P.H. Brookes.
Heath, Shirley Brice. (1983). *Ways with words: Language, life, and work in communities and classrooms*. Cambridge [Cambridgeshire]: Cambridge University Press.
Johnson, A., & Earle, T. (1987). *The evolution of human societies: From foraging group to agrarian state*. Stanford, CA: Stanford University Press.

Kernan, C. (1969). *The acquisition of language by Samoan children*. Unpublished Doctoral Dissertation, University of California at Berkeley. Cited in Brown (1973).

LeVine, S., & LeVine, R. (1981). Child abuse and neglect in Sub-Saharan Africa. In Jill E. Korbin (Ed.), *Abuse and neglect: Cross-cultural perspectives* (pp. 35–55). Berkeley, CA: University of California Press.

Ochs, E., & Schieffelin, B. (1995). The impact of socialization on grammatical acquisition. In P. Fletcher & B. MacWhinney (Eds.), *The handbook of child language* (pp. 73–94). Oxford, UK: Blackwell.

Ortner, S. B. (1981). Gender and sexuality in hierarchical societies: The case of Polynesia and some comparative implications. In S. B. Ortner & H. Whitehead (Eds.), *Sexual meanings: The cultural construction of gender and sexuality* (pp. 359–409). Cambridge: Cambridge University Press.

Piaget, J. (1997). *The language and thought of the child*. New York: Humanities Press.

Pollock, L. J. (2001). Parent–child relations. In D. I. Kertzer & M. Barbagli (Eds.), *Family life in early modern times 1500–1789* (pp. 191–220). New Haven, CT: Yale University Press.

Tolbert, M. K. (1978). *The acquisition of grammatical morphemes: A cross-linguistic study with reference to Mayan (Cakchikel) and Spanish*. Doctoral Dissertation, Harvard University, Cambridge, MA.

Wellman, H., & Gelman, S. (1998). Knowledge acquisition in foundational domains. In D. Kuhn & R. Siegler (Eds.), *The handbook of child psychology* (Vol. 2, 5th ed., pp. 523–574). New York: Wiley.

Whitehurst, G. J. (2001). *Address to the White House Summit on Early Childhood Cognitive Development*. Archived Information, July 26, U.S. Department of Education.

CONTRIBUTORS

Michelle M. Chouinard (Ph.D., 2005, Stanford University) is an Assistant Professor of Psychology at the University of California, Merced, where she is a Founding Faculty member. Her research investigates the role that conversation plays in cognitive development, with an emphasis on children's questions, language acquisition, and biological knowledge.

Paul Harris is a Developmental Psychologist with interests in the development of cognition, emotion, and imagination. After teaching at Oxford University for more than 20 years, he moved to Harvard University where he is currently Victor S. Thomas Professor of Education. He is a fellow of the British Academy and an emeritus fellow of St. John's College, Oxford. His latest book is *The Work of the Imagination* (Blackwell, 2000).

Michael Maratsos (Ph.D., 1972, Harvard University) is a Professor at the Institute of Child Development, University of Minnesota. His past interests were in language development. He is currently working on a book on the problem of resources, power, and developmental theory, using material from historical and anthropological sources in combination with psychological studies.

STATEMENT OF EDITORIAL POLICY

The *Monographs* series aims to publish major reports of developmental research that generate authoritative new findings and uses these to foster a fresh perspective or integration of findings on some conceptually significant issue. Submissions from programmatic research projects are welcomed; these may consist of individually or group-authored reports of findings from a single large-scale investigation or from a sequence of experiments centering on a particular question. Multiauthored sets of independent studies that center on the same underlying question may also be appropriate; a critical requirement in such instances is that the various authors address common issues and that the contribution arising from the set as a whole be unique, substantial, and well-integrated. Manuscripts reporting interdisciplinary or multidisciplinary research on significant developmental questions and those including evidence from diverse cultural, racial, ethnic, national, or other contexts are of particular interest. Because the aim of the series is not only to advance knowledge on specialized topics but also to enhance cross-fertilization among disciplines or subfields, the links between the specific issues under study and larger questions relating to developmental processes should emerge clearly for both general readers and specialists on the topic. In short, irrespective of how it may be framed, work that contributes significant data or extends developmental thinking will be considered.

Potential authors are not required to be members of the Society for Research in Child Development or affiliated with the academic discipline of psychology to submit a manuscript for consideration by the *Monographs*. The significance of the work in extending developmental theory and in contributing new empirical information is the crucial consideration.

Submissions should contain a minimum of 80 manuscript pages (including tables and references). The upper boundary of 150–175 pages is more flexible, but authors should try to keep within this limit. Please submit manuscripts electronically to the SRCD Monographs Online Submissions and Review Site (MONOSubmit) at www.srcd.org/monosubmit. Please contact the Monographs office with any questions at monographs@srcd.org.

The corresponding author for any manuscript must, in the submission letter, warrant that all coauthors are in agreement with the content of the manuscript. The corresponding author also is responsible for informing all coauthors, in a timely manner, of manuscript submission, editorial decisions, reviews received, and any revisions recommended. Before publication, the corresponding author must warrant in the submissions letter that the study was conducted according to the ethical guidelines of the Society for Research in Child Development.

Potential authors who may be unsure whether the manuscript they are planning would make an appropriate submission are invited to draft an outline of what they propose and send it to the editor for assessment. This mechanism, as well as a more detailed description of all editorial policies, evaluation processes, and format requirements, is given in the "Guidelines for the Preparation of Publication Submissions," which can be found at the SRCD website by clicking on *Monographs*, or by contacting the editor, W. Andrew Collins, Institute of Child Development, University of Minnesota, 51 E. River Road, Minneapolis, MN 55455-0345; e-mail: wcollins@umn.edu.

Monographs of the Society for Research in Child Development (ISSN 0037-976X), one of two publications of Society of Research in Child Development, is published three times a year by Blackwell Publishing with offices at 350 Main St., Malden, MA 02148 and PO Box 1354, Garsington Rd, Oxford, OX4 2DQ, UK and PO Box 378 Carlton South, 3053 Victoria, Australia. A subscription to *Monographs of the SRCD* comes with a subscription to *Child Development* (published bimonthly).

INFORMATION FOR SUBSCRIBERS For new orders, renewals, sample copy requests, claims, changes of address and all other subscription correspondences please contact the Journals Department at your nearest Blackwell office (address details listed above). UK office phone: +44 (0) 1865-778315, Fax: +44 (0) 1865-471775, Email: customerservices@ blackwellpublishing.com; US office phone: 800-835-6770 or 781-388-8599, Fax: 781-388-8232, Email: customerservices@blackwellpublishing.com; Asia office phone: +65 6511 8000, Fax: +61 3 8359 1120, Email: customerservices@blackwellpublishing.com

INSTITUTIONAL PREMIUM RATES* FOR MONOGRAPHS OF THE SRCD/CHILD DEVELOPMENT 2005 The Americas $471, Rest of World £335. Customers in Canada should add 7% GST to The Americas price or provide evidence of entitlement to exemption. Customers in the UK and EU should add VAT at 5% or provide a VAT registration number or evidence of entitlement to exemption.

*A Premium Institutional Subscription includes online access to full text articles from 1997 to present, where available. Print and online-only rates are also available.

BACK ISSUES Back issues are available from the publisher at the current single issue rate.

MICROFORM The journal is available on microfilm. For microfilm service, address inquiries to ProQuest Information and Learning, 300 North Zeeb Road, Ann Arbor, MI 48106-1346, USA. Bell and Howell Serials Customer Service Department: (800) 521-0600 × 2873.

MAILING Periodical postage paid at Boston, MA and additional offices. Mailing to rest of world by DHL Smart & Global Mail. Canadian mail is sent by Canadian publications mail agreement number 40573520. Postmaster: Send all address changes to *Monographs of the Society for Research in Child Development*, Blackwell Publishing Inc., Journals Subscription Department, 350 Main St., Malden, MA 02148-5020.

Sign up to receive Blackwell *Synergy* free e-mail alerts with complete *Monographs of the SRCD* tables of contents and quick links to article abstracts from the most current issue. Simply go to www.blackwell synergy.com, select the journal from the list of journals, and click on "Sign-up" for FREE email table of contents alerts.

CURRENT